The Spirit

Thames & Hudson

# of Asia

Journeys to the Sacred Places of the East

With 235 illustrations in colour

Photography by Michael Freeman

Text by Alistair Shearer

TITLE PAGES Shinto priests finish their morning prayers at Itsukushima-Jinja, Miyajima, Japan. HALF-TITLE PAGE Prayer flags hanging from a *bodhi* tree, Anuradhapura, Sri Lanka. ABOVE This banner with Dharmachakra is placed over the entrance to the Utse Samye Monastery, Yarking Valley, Tibet.

Designed by Rachida Zerroudi

First published in the United Kingdom in 2000 by
Thames & Hudson Ltd, 181A High Holborn, London WC1V 7QX

© 2000 Thames & Hudson Ltd, London
Specially commissioned photography © 2000 Michael Freeman
Text © 2000 Alistair Shearer

British Library Cataloguing-in-Publication Data
A catalogue record for this book is available from the British Library

ISBN 0-500-51023-7

Printed and bound in Spain by Graficas Reunidas S.A.

Contents

KAZAKSTAN

MONGOLIA

Tien Shan

Ürümqi
(Urumchi)

Tashkent

KYRGYZSTAN

Tarim

Gobi

Beijing
(Peking)

4

N. KOREA

Sea of
Japan

TAJIKISTAN

Takla Makan

C H I N A

Huang He

JAPAN

AFGHANISTAN

Kabul

Yellow
Sea

S. KOREA

Huang He

Zhengzhou

7 Kobe
36

6 Tokyo

Lahore

Indus

TIBET

Chang Jiang

Shanghai
35

PAKISTAN

18

Himalaya

3

32

34

Chang Jiang

Delhi

Tasangpo

Salween

(Yangtze Kiang)

NEPAL 10

33

9 31

30

BHUTAN

Kathmandu

Brahmaputra

8

Ganges

19

BANGLA-

I N D I A

DESH

Irrawaddy

MYANMAR
(BURMA)

Mekong

Guangzhou
(Canton)

TAIWAN

17

Nagpur

Kolkata
(Calcutta)

23 25

Hanoi

Mumbai
(Bombay)

Deccan

Godavari

Salween

L A O S

VIETNAM

26

Mekong

5

Yangon
(Rangoon) 24

13

THAILAND

PHILIPPINES

11 Chennai
(Madras)

Bangkok 27

14 29

South China Sea

12

CAMBODIA

Phnom Penh

20
21

Colombo 22 SRI
LANKA

BRUNEI

MALDIVES

MALAYSIA

I N D I A N

O C E A N

I N D O N E S I A

Jakarta

28 15 Surabaya

JAVA 2 16

0   500   1000 miles

0   500   1000   1500 kilometres

Key	
1	Adam's Peak
2	Gunung Agung
3	Mount Kailash
4	Tangyue Memorial Arches
5	Imperial Tombs of Perfume River
6	Ise-jingu
7	Miyajima
8	Varanasi
9	Pashupatinath
10	Nilakantha
11	Tiruvannamalai
12	Kanchipuram
13	Tirumala
14	Angkor Wat
15	Chandi Sukuh & Chandi Ceto
16	Bali
17	Shatrunjaya
18	Amritsar
19	Bodh Gaya
20	Anuradhapura
21	Polonnaruwa
22	Temple of the Tooth
23	Pagan
24	Shwedagon Pagoda
25	Sagaing
26	Si Satchanalai
27	Wat Phra Kaeo
28	Borobodur
29	Angkor Thom & Banteay Chhmar
30	Swayambhunath
31	Bodhnath
32	Samye
33	Tashilunpo
34	The Jokhang
35	Putuoshan
36	Koya-san

Introduction

Heaven on Earth

THIS BOOK IS A JOURNEY, both geographical and experiential. It traces the spread and manifestation of the perennial wisdom which has shaped the civilizations of the East. First observable in what the West calls 'animism' – a profound psychic sensitivity to the energies of the natural world – this root-wisdom matured into the sophisticated world views known as Hinduism and Buddhism, and blossomed into sites such as those celebrated in the following pages.

The most complete body of knowledge concerning the purpose, building, and effects of such sites is known as *Vastu Vidya*, 'the knowledge of the dwelling place'. Originating in remotest antiquity, it was passed down from generation to generation of specialized families in an unbroken oral tradition, being inscribed on palm-leaves only in the early Middle Ages in texts known as the *shilpa shastras*. *Vastu Vidya* covered all forms of architecture from hermit's hut to royal palace, from temple to city, and the

shastras stand as remarkably detailed and cogent blueprints of the ideal building. This sacred knowledge was carried, first by Hindu priests, later by Buddhist monks, wherever Indian civilization spread.

According to *Vastu Vidya*, architecture is a divine science, whose purpose is to create structures aligned to the universal Natural Law which silently upholds and nourishes all evolution. The overriding aim and necessity of human life is to live in accord with this Law (known in Sanskrit as *dharma*, in Chinese as *tao*); failure to do so will inevitably violate the ordered rhythms of climate, fertility, health and social cohesion. The result is suffering. Natural Law operates through myriad laws of nature, experienced and personified in the East as a celestial hierarchy of presiding spirits, gods and goddesses, which create the specific conditions that shape our nervous systems and give rise to the richly varied cultures through which human experience is organized. The sacred site is the place where, above all, we are brought

to reconnect with these causal energies and the cosmic intelligence they administer. As a microcosm of heaven on earth, the temple has the power to save humanity from becoming the greedy, blind and brutal agent of its own decline.

The *shastras* particularly encourage the building of sacred structures and praise the role of donor as a respected religious duty which, in tandem with the sacerdotal professions of builder, craftsman and artist, serve to elevate the whole society. That many sacred sites were also raised as testaments to a particular ruler in no way compromises their desired spiritual effect; indeed, the royal patron who acts to further *dharma* for himself and his people is said to enjoy the blessings of the gods. But while virtually no traces of royal buildings remain from early times, a breathtaking array of sacred sites, albeit in varying states of repair, still exists throughout the East. Their longevity is certainly due to the fact that the *shastras* specify that imperishable materials such as brick and stone be reserved for religious buildings, but it also stems from the fact that buildings constructed in accord with the eternal laws of nature are necessarily more durable.

To traditional peoples, culture is not just the optional production and consumption of pleasing artefacts, but a total disposition, and the disposition of Eastern cultures has always been to facilitate the

'It is said some being obstructed the earth and sky with its body.
The gods suddenly caught this being and laid it face down.
Whichever limbs were held by different gods
had those very gods as their presiding deities.
The Creator ordered that the being be the god of the building plot.'

BRIHAT SAMHITA

7

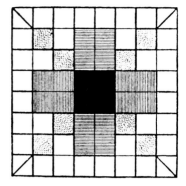 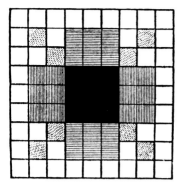

RIGHT Two examples of the *Vastu Mandala* ground plan, with sixty-four subdivisions (*left*) and eighty-one subdivisions (*right*).

experience of the sacred. Thus the temple, locus of education and the arts, inspiration and entertainment, is also the dream

place where time, the greatest enemy, is most easily transcended, and the deathless energy of the Divine floods into the world

humanity, the greater the stress in the atmosphere disturbing refined celestial influences. The soil is tested by each of the five senses: its smell, taste, colour, feel and even its sound when struck. Once the site has been judged acceptable, it is levelled by water, symbolizing the ocean of infinity from which the phenomenal world is constantly arising.

'Man follows the laws of earth;
earth follows the laws of heaven;
heaven follows the laws of Tao,
and Tao follows the laws of its own nature.'

TAO TE CHING

theatre in which the worshipper can safely encounter and integrate his inner world. The truly cultured person is not merely a knowledgeable consumer, but one who is conscious of all creation as the form of the Divine; for such a person, every act becomes a meaningful rite within the sacred drama we call life.

Whatever form the sanctuary takes – simple shrine, royal temple, sacred city – it is always the universal 'centre', the *bindu* ('seed point') at which creation is continually being born in inexhaustible freshness. From this infinite point radiate out the axes of time and space to create the material world. This theme is very naturally enacted in the process of building, and it is through architecture that we most perfectly mimic the Divine power whose agents, conscious or unwitting, we inevitably are. Conversely, as the place where heaven and earth most tangibly intersect, the sacred site is that

with least obstruction, to regenerate and renew.

As the cosmos is the extended environment in which we live, so the science and art of living in harmony with the celestial bodies is central to *Vastu Vidya*. The timing of key stages in the planning, construction and consecration of sacred buildings is determined according to planetary movements; each stage is accompanied by priestly rites connecting the built structure to the macrocosm. The schooled use of creative imagination in these rituals is crucial, for the East has long understood the power of awareness focused in meditation. Thought is the first impulse of the material expression of its object: as is the seed, so is the crop.

The site must be well placed. The land should be beautiful, and blessed with the fresh water and verdant trees conducive to angelic energies. Seclusion is also desirable: the greater the press of

In the next stage of construction a pillar is erected to symbolize the archetypal axis linking heaven and earth and a circle is drawn around it. In the Indian context, this cosmic pillar is the phallic *lingam* ('emblem') of Lord Shiva, pure Spirit, while the circle is the *yoni*, ('womb'; 'vagina') of Shakti Ma, the Great Goddess who is the material world. In China, similar rites invoked *yang*, the masculine principle imaged in sky, dragon and Emperor, and *yin*, the feminine principle embodied in earth, phoenix and Empress. Thus the birth of the temple re-enacts the primal creative union of complementary energies through which the cosmos comes into being.

The points where the pillar's shadow cuts the circle's circumference in the morning and evening give the East-West axis, then extrapolated into a square which becomes the site plan known as the *Vastu Mandala* (*above*), a microcosmic map of the universe subdivided into many smaller squares, each one governed by a presiding deity. Thus the totality of the universe is encapsulated in a two-dimensional plan, and the unlimited

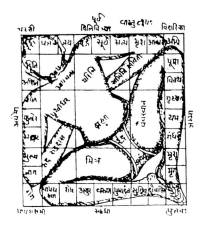

LEFT The *Vastu Purusha Mandala*, showing the temple as the microcosm of the universe, the Cosmic Man's self-sacrifice.

potential of the whole is made available in a limited physical structure. The central square (*brahmasthan*) is left empty as the source from which unmanifest intelligence pours forth to create matter. In the Hindu temple, this space is where the main image, the vehicle of the god, will be installed; in the Buddhist *stupa*, it is the sacred relic chamber. A particularly important site plan is the *Vastu Purusha Mandala* (*above*), which pictures the act of creation as the primordial self-sacrifice of Purusha, the Cosmic Man.

The next stage in laying out a site is right direction. This is determined by the path of the sun, which as the source of all light, life and intelligence, is the supreme embodiment of Natural Law for our planet. Derived from the sun, each of the cardinal points and mid-points has its own particular energy and influence. Sanctuaries should face East to absorb each morning's new vitality; their buildings and rituals should be correlated to the sun's path.

Within the articulated site, the transition from outer to inner is always a delicate process, carefully protected to avoid the intrusion of negative influences. Guardians oversee the vulnerable points – entrances, exits, intersections – of what is a living organism. Corners too are potential weaknesses: externally they disrupt linear symmetry, internally they are repositories of negative energy. Only when all its angles are protected can the sanctuary act as a reception hall fit to entertain the celestial energies.

Then comes proportion. As in the associated arts of music and mathematics, architecture employs a limited vocabulary of forms in various combinations and on various scales. Repetition engenders a subliminal, cumulative effect of coherence by not taxing eye and brain with too much variety. Here sacred art mimics nicely the workings of Nature, which is endlessly creative in engendering subtly different variations of prototypical forms – cell, snowflake or flower. It is through correct proportion that the plastic tension of matter is harmonized with the incorruptible geometry of spirit.

In their celebration of a continuity of belief and practice that has proven efficacy, these sacred sites are essentially conservative, even nostalgic. The individual talent of architect or artist has true worth only when aligned to this tradition as its freshest exponent – individualism, so trumpeted in the cliques of contemporary Western art, has no place here. Oblivious to fashion, sacred art sees no need of radical or febrile adjustment merely to serve transient ideologies of novelty or 'progress'. From its perspective, it is the lack of a stable and guiding metaphysic, prevalent in a civilization divorced from Nature, that allows the secular commercialism which is the death of true creativity. Yet sacred art is by no means rigidly fixed. The generic unity of sacred sites such as those which follow is very often given individual character by richly embellished detail, inside and out. The Sanskrit word for such detail is *samskara* – 'refinement' – a word rich in associations applied to various cultured skills: education, jewellery-making, the presentation of food. In Oriental psychology the term is somewhat analogous to the Western concept of 'the unconscious', and describes the residual impressions of past experience which, giving rise to habitual patterns of perception and behaviour, determine and condition our present life. It is thus our *samskaras* that structure our fragile human uniqueness, rendering the universal individual, the species particular. Similarly, the individuality of any sacred building lies partly in the way it is lovingly fashioned as a specific and precious variation on an unending and universal theme.

ABOVE The morning view from Chiu Gompa towards Mount Kailash, Lake Manasarovar, Tibet. OPPOSITE Pilgrims pass a sacred boulder on their circumambulation of Kailash.

GUARDIANS

FIRST COMES THE EARTH, ancient mother of the gods, intrinsically holy, irrepressible womb of the Divine. Then, here and there across the landscape simple shrines spring up, separating and protecting what is particularly holy ground: that place, be it mountain, tree or rock, where the invisible presences that govern our world are known to congregate, where they have been felt or seen, either in direct revelation, or by their witnessed effects. Some miraculous event, a punishment, healing or a vision, shows that the hidden forces are breathing through such a place,

bending the commonplace boundaries of time and space and infusing them with a numinous power that puts the visitor in contact with new levels of being. The site of such an epiphany becomes first a place of pilgrimage, then the hub of a community. People settle nearby to imbibe the energy; ritual specialists – healers, soothsayers, dancers, shamans – gather to perform their arts, and the tools of their sacred trade – masks, drums, talismans – are left at the site of the shrine, to guard and absorb its magical power.

OF THE WORLD
The Forces of Nature

Little by little the shrine grows and attracts the attention of the rich and powerful. A local chieftain prays for the continuance of his family or for success in battle. Fortune smiles on him; he raises an altar in thanksgiving. In time other patrons come; leaf and branch are replaced by wood and stone. A permanent building rises up, perhaps long after the original reason for sanctity has been forgotten. Later, a visiting teacher decides to found a temple; its longevity and influence will reflect the purity of his consciousness.

But however sophisticated the temple may become, it continues, rather than replaces, the shrine, even though it may in time come to serve ends other than the immediate apprehension of the mysterious divine. To the devout there is no conflict between the two; the motley, impromptu heaps and mounds of the poor continue to exist happily in the shadow of even the most refined and articulate structures. And both deserve attention, for the gods can be fickle, and who really knows where they will deign to appear and how they will demand to be honoured?

Waters of Life
Sacred Springs

WATER IS THE MOTHER OF CIVILIZATION, as fire is its father. Early cultures naturally clustered on the banks of the great Asian arterial waterways – Indus, Ganges, Yangtze, and dozens of others – using the precious substance for drinking, washing, cooking, and irrigation as well as healing and ritual purposes. Thus religion fits into a natural cycle linking human and divine: from rain comes rice, from rice comes wealth, from wealth comes patronage, from patronage comes worship and from worship comes rain. But Mother Nature can withhold as well as give, or give too abundantly, and many of the sites in this book owe their existence to the painstaking engineering necessary to manage water and outwit the vagaries of drought and flood. The ancient civilizations of Sri Lanka and above all, Cambodia, were particularly skilled in creating systems of storage and distribution that have never been bettered.

Water is life. It has always been seen as a gift of the gods by both sea-faring and landlocked Asia, a necessity that is itself divine. Many rivers are considered sacred to this day, especially in India, where their water is believed to have healing powers. The Sanskrit word for a pilgrimage spot is *tirtha*, meaning 'ford', and the confluence of two rivers is especially holy. This reverence for water is found throughout Asia: in Thailand a river is called *mae* ('mother'); in Bhutan streams are used to turn giant prayer wheels; the Tibetans read omens from images in their sacred lakes, while the ancient Khmers had their rivers flowing over images of the gods to empower the water and ensure the health of the crops.

Water is the supremely feminine element: nourishing, slow, lunar, adaptable, always able to find its own level and imbued with the invincible strength of patience – a single drop repeated often enough

'When unleashed, the mighty waters generated the mother of all...
from there was the one life-breath of the gods breathed forth.'

RIG VEDA

OPPOSITE AND THIS PAGE
Sacred springs, marked by votive offerings, occur throughout the East: the spring at Yeh Pulu, Bedulu, Bali (*left* and *opposite*); floral offerings at the source of the Cauvery river, Karnataka, India.

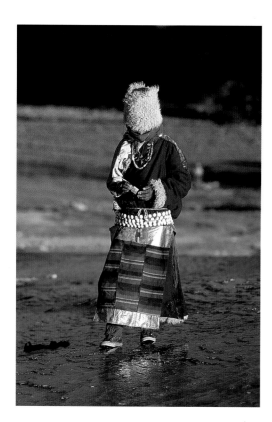

ABOVE AND OPPOSITE
Rutok pilgrims gather
at the sacred hot
springs of Tirthapuri,
Ngari Province, Tibet, to
drink the sacred water.

Sacred Springs

will cut through the hardest stone. Flowing downwards from its crystalline source, its purity becoming gradually clouded by the earth it passes through, water is a perfect analogy to the Divine radiance, increasingly obscured by its own material creation. The almost sacramental status afforded water by traditional societies is due to an instinctual affinity we humans feel with the substance. All life originated from the sea; we spend the first nine months of our life floating in water; our bodies are ninety per cent water, and we live on a watery planet. This last is particularly so, of course, for those who live in tropical or semi-tropical climes; no one who has not experienced a monsoon can imagine its primal power. Even today in those parts of the Orient where villagers living on or by water move home with the monsoon tide – perhaps six or seven times a year – it is possible to witness the ancient yet vital relationship our species has always enjoyed with water, in sacred, economic, dangerous and pleasurable ways.

It is in everyday religious ritual that this intimate relationship with water is most charmingly expressed. Hindu images are lovingly lustrated with sacred water, and other watery liquids – milk, ghee, honey, coconut juice; Buddha images receive bowls of water as offerings, and the naturally adaptable flowing of water is seen as the ideal mode of behaviour for the Taoist sage. The potent combination of racial memory and everyday reality made it inevitable that water would play a central role in the earliest mythologies. In Hinduism, the Golden Egg, seed of all manifestation, emerges from the primal waters to generate cycle after cycle of creation, in Chinese myth the world rests on a giant turtle floating on the heavenly waters, while the Buddhists picture the various universes as fabulous islands rising out of the cosmic sea.

Sacred Stones
Nature's Markers

STONES ARE THE FIRST MONUMENTS, marking out the points of holiness on the earth, charting our relationship with the heavens. From neolithic times they stand, mute testaments to our urgent need, beyond any pedestrian measure of effort or money, to state our place in the surrounding enormity. The one creation of nature that abides, stones are magically dependable, optimistically proclaiming stability amidst the constant flux of life.

Throughout the East, two types of stones predating figurative images have traditionally been the focus of widespread devotion. First come the 'naturally occurring' (*swayambhu*), single slabs or outcrops of rock that are considered highly numinous. In Japan, the indigenous Shinto faith adorns piles of such stones (*otsuka*) with sacred straw ropes hung with cloth or paper strips to show their sanctity. The Gardens of Longevity of Chinese Taoism celebrate the permanence of stone, while both Chan and Zen Buddhist monasteries make stones the central feature of meticulously raked sand gardens. Stones may spontaneously resemble a seated Buddha, the head of Ganesha or vulva of the Great Goddess. A special catagory of places where the celestial energies have left their mark on earth is the 'footprint' (*pada*). These may be associated with the Hindu god Vishnu, or enlightened beings like Buddha, whose 'footprints' are everywhere in south-east Asia.

The spiritual energy of stone may announce itself in the recondite forms of ammonite fossils (*shalagrama*) found in India's holy Narmada river and deemed sacred to Vishnu, or spin the swirling spirals in agate, tiger's eye or sea-shells, to create a natural mandala, a microcosmic indicator of the cosmic rhythms of involution and evolution. Many of the principal images in the most important Hindu temples are simple unworked lumps of stone or rock, too holy to carve or alter, and all over the East, smaller stones of many types serve as amulets and talismans, portable power-seeds invested with the subtle strength of faith.

Then there are the man-made, but still abstract representations. Most widespread is the Hindu *lingam* ('emblem') that stands for the unmanifest power of Shiva who, as Lord of Transformation, is the embodiment of the invincible evolutionary energy. Sometimes the *lingam* is shaped as a phallus, erect and stable, potent with unshed seed; often it is grasped by the *yoni* ('womb' or 'vagina') of the great goddess Shakti, the enduring material energy. Together, they represent the eternally complementary principles of masculine and feminine, spirit and matter, and they are found wherever Hinduism spread. A similar archetype is expressed in the Buddhist relic mound (*stupa*).

OPPOSITE AND LEFT
Natural markers of holy places in Japan: Meoto-Iwa ('married rocks'), Futami (*far left*), and the sacred rock of Waroza-ishi (*left*), inscribed with Sanskrit characters.

The Sacred Tree
Linking Heaven and Earth

IT STANDS UNMOVING AT THE CENTRE of the universe, joining earth and heaven, yet keeping each in its rightful, preordained place. As the eternal *axis mundi* it is the stable pillar around which the myriad ever-changing worlds revolve. Its branches, stretching to all infinity, offer impartial protection to beings without number, while its prehensile roots, binding the fertile earth in place, draw from the inexhaustible freshness of life itself.

It is the Sacred Tree, oldest and deepest of archetypes, found in all cultures at all times. As the symbol of life itself, our covenant with the Divine, the Sacred Tree takes many forms – as Tree of Life, Tree of Wisdom, Tree of Knowledge – its ancient rhizome sprouting in countless axes linking heaven and earth, from totem pole to church spire. So universal is this symbol, may it not embody a species memory of that fateful day some six million years ago when, somewhere on the African savannah, our primate ancestors swung down from the branches and began to walk as upright as the tree itself? And, much later, it was the forest, its clearings fed by twisting paths, that was the blueprint of our cities with streets and alleys leading to open squares and green spaces, alongside which the vaulted ceilings of assembly rooms and cathedrals harked back to overarching boughs.

To be linked to the invisible worlds each village had its sacred tree in which the presiding spirit lived, a shrine set up in its shade. The village headman, local representative of cosmic order, would sit under the tree to dispense justice and favour, and when he moved it moved with him, in the form of a protective parasol carried by an attendant. Tree and parasol became intertwined as symbols of royalty and divinity, as they still are all over the East today: ceremonial parasols protect offerings as they are carried to the temple in Bali, they shelter senior monks in Japan and *pontiffs* in India, while in Thailand they rise in ascending tiers above the thrones of both Buddha and king.

Each of the liberated saints (*tirthankaras*) of Jainism is associated with his tree, and the four cardinal points of the Buddha's life – his birth, *nirvana*, first teaching and death – all take place under the sacred tree. Long before Buddhism, the archetypal ascetic Shiva sat under the holy *ashwattha* to teach yoga, his long tresses as tangled as its serpentine aerial roots. And serpents are very much part of the story, for where trees are found termites will build their conical nests in the shade, and where termites are found, hungry snakes will gather. This combination of snake and tree, actual and symbolic, is again universal. Long ago the Semitic desert world mythologized it in a distant oasis called Eden, but all over tropical Asia it is still found as a vital part of a folk awareness which worships trees as living beings and homes of spirits – hanging them with coloured threads and garlands, daubing them with paint and powder, lustrating them with holy water.

*'The Tree of Life comprises all the worlds; none ever goes beyond it. Varuna,
lord of the waters, sustains the tree erect. Its rays of light stream downward.
Deep may they sink within us and be hidden.'*

RIG VEDA

OPPOSITE AND LEFT
Prayers at tree shrines: a woman and child at Venugopalaswamy Temple, dedicated to Krishna near Mysore, Karnataka, India; *Nat* (guardian spirit) shrines around a tree, Bhamo, Kachin State, Burma.

Linking Heaven and Earth

The Sacred Tree is preeminently the
life–giver. In India its branches are strung
with red cords or miniature cradles by
women who long for children. After her
wish has been granted the grateful mother
will return to place a little cloth bundle
containing the placenta on a branch.
Stones carved with snakes are set up
among tree roots – infertility in this life is
deemed the result of having killed a snake
in a previous one – and trees, particularly
the *banyan* and *peepul* (two species of
inedible fig), are often 'married': planted
in a walled shrine where they grow to
intertwine as the embodiments of Vishnu
and his consort Lakshmi, or Radha and her
divine lover Krishna. In China the
medicinal *ginko* tree – a 'silver apricot' –
was cultivated in temples and monasteries
and believed to protect the buildings from
fire.

The Sacred Tree as *kalpa vrisksha*,
'Granter of all Treasures' (unconsciously
celebrated in the pagan Christmas tree
ritual of the West), was majestically
depicted in the stone reliefs of the great
Javanese temples – Hindu Prambanan,
Buddhist Borobodur – over twelve
hundred years ago; it is enlivened to this
day in the 'money trees', branches hung
with banknotes, offered at Chinese and
Tibetan altars. In the esoteric teachings of
yoga, *kalpa vriksha* is internalized, to
symbolize the many-branched human
nervous system. It is this model of subtle
physiology on which Oriental systems of
healing, such as acupuncture, are based.
Now the spiritual energy (*kundalini*) lies
coiled like a snake at the base of the spine;
as she uncoils and rises through the
sushumna nerve embedded in the core of
the spinal cord, she purifies the entire
subtle body. When fully purified, the
nervous system is able to dispense the
greatest of all treasures – Enlightenment.

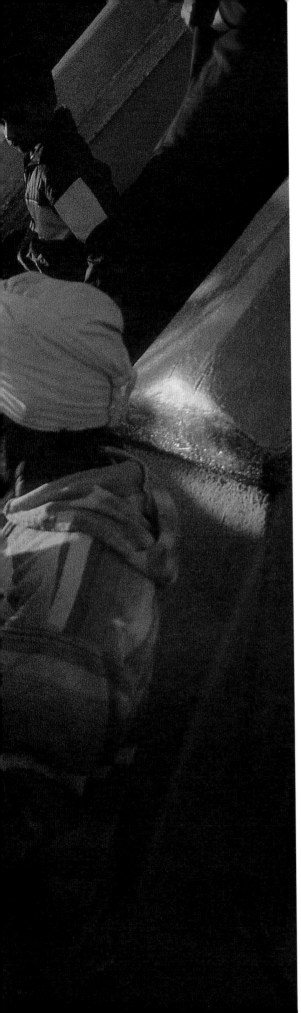

The Sacred Mountain
Axis Mundi

MOUNTAINS ARE ESPECIALLY HOLY. As the point where mother earth stretches up to eagerly to meet father sky, and the celestial energies reach languorously down to bless the human realm, they are the fertile ground of high and low, where human meets Divine. As such they are the preferred dwelling place of the deities, where they hold their courts and grant audience, dispensing favour and punishment alike.

To take but one example, China. From the Zhou dynasty of 1000 B.C. right through until the end of the Ching Dynasty in A.D. 1912, the Emperor always prayed to the sacred mountains at special altars to ensure the well-being and prosperity of the state. Shunning such centralized authority, the anarchic sages of Taoism, a potent spiritual force from at least A.D. 200 onwards, envisaged the sacred mountain as the abode of the Immortals, and thus the place most favourable to the discovery of the elusive elixir of immortality. More soberly, patriarchal Confucian scholars saw the lofty peaks as paradigms of world order, far removed from the disorderly conduct of man. Such themes are drawn from our common imagination – Sinai, Olympus and Athos tell the same story in the West – and ancient architectural texts the world over consistently cite the mountain as the most auspicious place to build shrine, temple or monastery.

Other more abstract and universal levels of symbolic resonance derive from the very physicality of the mountain. Vertical, it is the *axis mundi*, established as the stable pivot around which the universe revolves. Massive and unmoving, it represents that which transcends change, the still point at the very centre of the evolving universe. This adamantine stability – the word *achala* means both 'mountain' and 'unmoving' in Sanskrit – is the very essence of the Absolute ground of life, the unmoving mover of all fleeting phenomena, and as such aligns the mountain to the sacred centre from which all manifestation emerges, and into which it eventually returns. As the navel of creation inverted, the mountain is also the horizontal axis, grounding the gathered creative cosmic energy and radiating it out in all directions.

Remote and rugged, the mountain is always a place of existential intensity. It stands as a challenge to test the bold or the foolhardy, whose achievements may be glorious but whose hubris is mocked and punished, sometimes by death. As such, the mountain is an apt metaphor for the spiritual quest as a journey from the humdrum valley of everyday life to the rarified heights of liberation. Each traveller on the climb will have a different view according to how far towards the summit he has progressed, and in the ascending hierarchy of wisdom each teaching is provisional, a perspective from whichever stage has so far been reached. This is why the Sanskrit for 'philosophy' is *darshana* ('a point of view') and one of the commonest epithets for the elevated status of the Enlightened is *kutashtha*: 'he who is established on the peak'.

LEFT Ritual circumambulation (*pradakshina*) at sunrise around the summit of Adam's Peak, Sri Lanka.

The Sacred Mountain: *Adam's Peak, Sri Lanka*

WHEN ADAM was thrown out of the paradise he landed here; it was here that Lord Vishnu made his descent from the celestial heaven of Vaikuntha. Here too the Buddha, practising teleportation, arrived to bring the *dharma*, and even Mohammed was here to preach his austere desert doctrine. Whichever religion you ascribe to, this mountain is its apex, the zenith of its myth. At 7500 feet high, Adam's Peak is not the highest mountain in Sri Lanka, but it is the island's most spiritually elevated spot, a unifying cosmic centre that serves the needs of all its variegated communities. As such, it celebrates an ancient, intrinsic holiness – the spirit of place – lively long before the historical religions began their interminable squabbling.

Sri Pada ('The Sacred Footprint'), as it is known locally, draws pilgrims all the year round. Each full moon day (*poya*) is traditionally the time for 20,000 or more to make the ascent, culminating in a sighting (*darshan*) of the 'footprint' – a three-foot-long indentation in the natural rock. The mountain has spawned its own traditions. First-time climbers will wear white turbans; people pause at the 'place of the needle' to toss a threaded needle into a sacred bush at the spot where the Buddha is believed to have paused to mend his robe; pilgrims passing each other limit their conversation to '*karuvanai, karuvanai*!' – 'Peace be with you'.

The traditional route is a seven-hour climb which starts from above Ratnapura, the island's gem capital, and winds through lush estates of rubber and paddy on the edge of the island's central tea growing area. It is busiest from late December to April, before the spring monsoons, when the sky is clear enough for unclouded vistas. The ascent is begun in time to arrive before dawn, and follows a snaking path which the kings of Sri Lanka punctuated with rest-houses.

The climb is freezing, but the view at first light, stretching over the hills to the east and westwards to the sea, is more than ample reward. But the most magical sight is to come. As the sun rises, an incandescent ball unpeeling layers of turquoise, pink and orange, it casts the long triangular shadow of the peak on to the surrounding clouds. As it rises, so the shadow hovers as a natural hologram, before beginning to curve back into its own misty base, finally to disappear into open space. It is an extraordinary spectacle; little wonder the faithful have always seen it as a sign of some higher power gracing our world. They have given that power many different names – Jehovah, Vishnu, Allah – but it is the ball of liquid light which endures, dawn after dawn; all else is but a passing show.

ABOVE AND OPPOSITE
Sunrise over Adam's Peak, Sri Lanka: worshippers on the summit salute the sun; the otherworldly shadow of the mountain is projected over the surrounding clouds as the sun rises.

The Sacred Mountain: *Gunung Agung, Bali*

GUNUNG AGUNG, the semi-active volcano, is the *axis mundi* of the Balinese world, where the elemental forces of sky, sacred mountain and fire all meet. Above this smouldering peak is the celestial home of the creator Shiwaditya, who incorporates two major Hindu deities – Shiva and the sun-god Aditya – and below him live the various other gods. Among these are counted the divine ancestors of the Balinese people, and it is they who own the land.

This slumbering giant last erupted in 1963, the year of the most sacred of all festivals, Eka Dasa Rudra. Performed roughly every hundred years to placate Rudra, the great god Shiva in his fierce form, this celebration traditionally

ABOVE AND RIGHT
A split-gate (*chandi bentar*) sunrise, Pura Pasar Agung, Gunung Agung, Bali; sunset beyond Gunung Agung, from Ahmed, on Bali's east coast.

demands that one of every species on the island, from ant to man, should be offered into the rumbling crater.

Set on the slopes of Gunung Agung is Bali's 'Mother temple', Besakih. Thus Besakih is no great architectural wonder, but a series of large ramshackle courtyards, housing over 200 structures strung with sacred parasols and pendants and arranged into about forty temples and shrines. There is no feeling here of order imposed from without; rather the whole place seems to go on by itself, the humans playing no more intrusive role than any other aspect of the natural world. Each temple has the tiered roofs of a *meru* – a symbolic amalgam of the cosmic mountain and sacred tree – which must always be an odd number. Though the Mother Goddess is incarnated in Dewi Shri, the benign and nourishing rice deity celebrated in paddy-field shrines and colourful festivals throughout the island, there is something quite impenetrable about Besakih for the visitor. This is not only due to the disorientating lack of order of the shrines, but stems from something deeper than the physical. Set at 950 metres above sea level, the place is often covered in damp, misty cloud that descends from the mountain, giving it a strange, ghostly atmosphere.

Surprisingly, or perhaps not, Besakih suffered little damage despite its proximity to the crater. Annulled by the eruption, which shattered south-east Bali, destroying crops and rendering thousands homeless, the Eka Dasa Rudra ceremony was finally performed successfully in 1979. But the legacy of the great God's wrath is still apparent if one approaches the mountain from the north-east coastal plains. Here the savage side of Gunung Agung appears unabashed, rising monumentally up from the foothills over which its debris is strewn.

The Sacred Mountain: *Mount Kailash, Tibet*

THE HIGH ALTITUDE DESERT that is the isolated Ngari region of western Tibet is a wild, merciless place. A vast lunar expanse swept by vicious and unrelenting winds, it is peopled only by the occasional band of hardy nomadic herdsmen, tiny dots beneath a sky of breathtaking luminosity and awe-inspiring magnitude. The place is as empty and as silent as the end of the world. The air here is so thin the senses are peeled: colours have an hallucinatory intensity, every object glowing with its own light, and you can hear the sugar dissolve in your tea. In such surroundings our petty human preoccupations pale into insignificance; no wonder the Tibetans live in commune with the fierce elemental forces. The barrier between the seen and unseen worlds feels wafer-thin in Ngari, our mundane laws of time and space transcended.

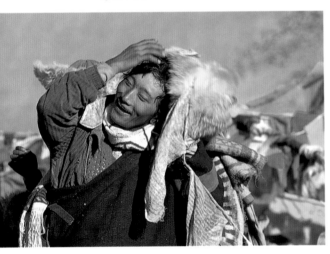

ABOVE AND OPPOSITE
Pilgrims gather at the sacred rock of Phawang Megar, Drolma La, the highest point in the circumambulation of Mount Kailash, lifting the lines of banners of sacred texts.

Out of this primeval landscape rises a 22,028-foot-high rock pyramid capped in snow. It is the most sacred mountain in the world. To the indigenous shamanistic people of Shang-Shung this adamantine rock was 'The Place of the Nine-tiered Swastika', while Hindus know it as Kailash, the abode of Shiva, Lord of Transformation, who dwells here with his wife Parvati, 'Lady of the Mountain'. To the Buddhists it is Kang Rimpoche, 'Precious Snow Mountain', the throne of their terrifying tutelary deity Demchog, while the Jains call it Ashtapada, 'The Eight Steps', on the summit of which Adinath, the founder of their ancient faith, attained enlightenment. Of all the pilgrimage places in Asia it is the holiest; one circuit of its thirty-two mile circumambulatory path is believed to wipe out the bad *karma* of a lifetime. But such grace does not come easily; each year the unpredictable weather claims lives of pilgrim and tourist alike.

The appeal of Kailash has not been limited to believers; over the last three hundred years many Westerners have fallen under its spell. The first to travel across the 'vast, sterile and terrible desert' that is Western Tibet was the intrepid Italian Jesuit Ippolito Desideri in 1715; the rigours of his journey, that even today is two weeks' hard travel from Lhasa, are vividly described in his writings. Later, European explorers would trek here, fascinated by rumours that the iridescent turquoise waters of the sacred lake Manasarovar, not far from Kailash, were the source of the four great rivers that water India: the Brahmaputra, Indus, Sutlej and Karnali.

It was not until 1907 that the Swede Sven Hedlin, the first European to circumambulate the mighty mountain, confirmed what folk tales had long described. The preeminent religious

importance of Kailash stems from the fact that it is the physical form of another, subtler peak: the celestial Mount Meru. A place of unimaginable power, Meru is the archetypal sacred mountain, existing for all eternity as the navel of the universe. Meru is often called Sumeru, and in our age, legends about it may well have originated somewhere between 3500 and 2000 B.C. in the Mesopotamian cities of Sumeria, whose people mimicked it in their stepped ziggurats. But whatever its earliest references, Meru has long dominated the imagination of the Orient, and is found from India to Japan, from Central Asia to Java. It was known in China since around 1000 B.C. as Mount Kunlun, and all the faiths of the East have described it in their sacred texts and

ABOVE AND RIGHT
Pilgrim *chortens* (*stupas*) close to Mount Kailash, embellished with yak skulls, horns and prayer flags; in the background looms the north face of the mountain.

myths, pictured it in their cosmological diagrams, symbolized it in the towers, domes and spires of their sacred buildings. Epigraphs of the Khmers of Cambodia, to take but one among countless examples, specifically describe their temples as 'the Golden Mountain' or 'King of the Mountains'.

The *Vishnu Purana*, a seminal Hindu text from about 200 B.C., describes Meru in glowing terms as rising a majestic 84,000 leagues at the centre of the universe, encircled by the concentric rings of the seven oceans and the seven continents. The four directions radiate out from its four luminous faces of crystal, lapis lazuli, ruby and gold, and the myriad tiers of 'the three worlds' – heaven, earth and the underworld – rotate around this axial pivot. Here too are ordered the sun, moon and stars, whose stately processions ceaselessly influence human and cosmic life. From the peak of the mountain cascades a living stream of water, dividing into four to nourish the four quarters of the earth.

LEFT AND ABOVE Pilgrims gather at Chuku Gompa, Mount Kailash, spinning portable and fixed prayer wheels to send the spiritual influence of the texts to all corners of the universe.

Appeasing the Owners
Spirit Houses, Thailand

ASK THE TYPICAL THAI why his life is going well and the chances are that he will point to a curious structure, looking something like a cross between a bird-table and an exotic doll's-house, standing in the corner of his garden or compound. This is a spirit house (*wat phra non*), the residence of Phra Phum, 'the Lord of the Place', the presiding spirit of the area. Spirit houses are found everywhere in the kingdom, and are the most widespread manifestation of the country's vibrant animistic life. If anyone erects a building, they must provide alternative accommodation for the displaced spirit, for it is he who is the rightful owner of the place.

Phra Phum is only one of the vast pantheon of spirits (*phi*) that populate the Thai universe. Many of these, especially the destructive ones, are female, and particularly in the countryside, may lurk in certain types of fruit or tree, or at a crossroads, in order to surprise their victims. They all belong to the psychic realm the Thais designate as *decha* – a realm of chaos far from the safety of home, temple or monastery, where potentially destructive powers roam at will causing harm, loss, illness or death. Such random forces can only be tamed by

the skills of the village spirit-doctor, or the special class of magically gifted monks who act as white magicians or exorcists when the need arises. Thus it is not uncommon to see clusters of spirit houses beside the road at a particularly dangerous bend or accident black spot, set up to protect the traveller. If placated sufficiently Phra Phum, as well as bestowing a generally benign presence, can bless particular and important events of everyday life.

Phra Phum's residence is found in a considerable range of designs. The grandest are miniature palaces in wood and cement that, with their stepped roofs, gilded spires, mirror-encrusted façades and carefully carved doors and window-sills, resemble miniature Buddhist temples, while the simplest are ramshackle bamboo huts found in the poor upcountry areas or the slums of Bangkok. Though each house is unique, the basic structure is always the same: a room in which Phra Phum lives, and a portico or veranda on which the daily offerings of food, fresh flowers, incense sticks, garlands and water are placed. He should also be provided with objects, such as a retinue of miniature servants, horses, elephants or cattle; these will make the inhabitant feel

'*Every man should be skilled in the art of drinking tea,
drinking liquor, eating and making love...*'

THAI HILL TRIBE MOTTO

OPPOSITE AND RIGHT
This Thai spirit house has been constructed around a tree in Mae Hong Son, outside Wat Phra Non monastery; Bangkok shops sell small statues to attend the Lord of Place in his shrine.

at home in a way that befits his status. The ancient fertility beliefs adhering to this custom can be seen at some spirit houses, where the main offerings are phalluses sculpted in wood, wax or stone, ranging in size from a few inches to three or four feet.

Spirit houses always stand level with, or slightly higher than, a person of average height, and are installed with an elaborate consecration ceremony lasting perhaps three hours. As an echo of Indian influence in the country, this is always performed by a *brahmin* priest, not a Buddhist monk, at the astrologically auspicious time. If, however, things are not going well for the owner of the compound, an expert who normally belongs to a special class of monk may be called in to question the spirit as to why it is unhappy and perform the necessary appeasement rituals. Such beliefs are not only found in the isolated country areas. In an open-mindedness typical of the Orient, even the most sophisticated hotels and westernized offices in downtown Bangkok ascribe their good fortune to the invisible occupant of the spirit house in their grounds.

ABOVE AND OPPOSITE
The usual location for a spirit house is around a *bodhi* tree: examples at Wat Ched Yod, Chiangmai, and at Wat Ko Kaeo, Sutharam, Petchaburi.

Guardian Spirits
The Nats *of Burma*

FOR THE EIGHT DAYS LEADING UP to the August full moon each year the village of Taungbyon, 20 kilometres north of Mandalay, is a frenzy of celebration. Impromptu altars are everywhere, fluttering gilt and tinsel and bearing offerings; uproarious processions stagger around the huge temporary bazaar, pilgrims peeling off to enjoy ceremonial dances, consultations with visiting shamans and healers, and the virtually incessant eating, drinking and gambling. Every so often the excitement rises to fever pitch as two wooden figures are paraded through the crowd which ebbs and flows in its efforts to touch them. These are the Brother Lords, two important members of the pantheon of thirty-seven protective spirits (*nats*) that govern the life of the Burmese, and it is in their honour that this holy fairground is taking place.

The tale of the Lords is a sorry one. Their father, a Muslim miracle worker who aided King Anawrahta in the conquest of Thaton in A.D. 1044, was rewarded with the role of Royal Flower Officer. But he fell in love with an ogress who lived on the sacred Mount Popa, and was executed because he spent his time with her instead of providing his master with fresh flowers each day. His two sons, taken into the king's service, must have inherited their father's love of idleness, for when a *pagoda* was being built here at Taungbyon, they chose to play marbles rather than participate; they too lost their lives for such insolence. As a consolation, they became the Brother Lords.

Such tragic tales are common in the genealogy of the *nats*; perhaps because of this they are by and large a vindictive lot, jealous of attention and needing recognition and appeasement if life is to proceed smoothly. For this reason every Burmese pays them great respect and some, like Bo Bo Gyi who guards the mighty Shwedagon Pagoda, have been given jobs of national responsibility. Burma is irredeemably animistic, and when the Buddhist monks arrived they sensibly incorporated the indigenous spirit worship into their teaching.

Originally, the pantheon of *nats* seems to have numbered thirty-six, sporting colourful names such as Lady Golden Sides, the Lord with the White Umbrella, The Lady Bandy Legs, and the Old Man by the Solitary Banyan Tree. It was Anawrahta, at whose request the Buddhist monks had brought their new religion, who cleverly instituted a thirty-seventh

OPPOSITE AND LEFT
A view of Mount Popa, the holy mountain of the *nats*, near Pagan, Burma; *nats* appear as figurines in various forms, each with its colourful legends. One here (far left) is accompanied by the auspicious leogryph (*chinthe*).

The Nats *of Burma*

Thagyamin, to act as the king of the *nats*.
He let it be known that this new addition
was also a worshipper of the Buddha. His
people were happy to follow suit, and to
this day the typical Burmese has no
difficulty in offering his allegiance to both
the Buddha and the *nat* guardians. Thus
the lunar month of Nadaw
(November/December) is officially
dedicated to *nat* festivals around the
country; followed by Pyato
(December/January) which belongs to
Buddhist temple festivals.

It was smart thinking on the part of an
earlier king, Thinlikyaung, who ruled in
the 4th century, that established the
national status of the two most revered
nats. A young blacksmith, Mr. Handsome
Face, and his sister, Golden Face, were
murdered by a wicked king. The two spirits
took up their abode in a tree and became
nats, dedicating themselves to causing
mischief in the king's court. When he
learned of their hiding place, the ruler had
the tree chopped down and thrown into
the nearby Irrawaddy river.

Downstream, Thinlikyaung's glance fell
on the tree as it floated past. Hearing the
story behind it, he had it carved into two
forms, and brother and sister were taken
ceremoniously to the sacred Mount Popa,
from where they reign until this day, as
the Mahagiri *nats* (Great Mountain Spirits).
This volcanic stub lies about 50 kilometres
south-east of Pagan rising over 1500
metres above the vast dry plain; the
Mahagiri shrine is about half-way up the
mountain. Between the 4th and 11th
centuries it served as a state oracle, each of
the kings of Pagan coming here to consult
it on his coronation. The place is a tranquil
spot with a breathtaking view; nothing
disturbs its monasteries until the month of
Nayon (May/June) when, with the annual
Festival of Spirits, the crowds pour in and
the sacred carnival starts once more.

Gateways to Other Worlds
Hill-tribe Shrines of Thailand

THE THRESHOLD, that place which divides the pure inner world from the impure outer, is always delicate. The safe familiarity of the house, village or tribe must be protected from what is unknown and potentially hostile; places of special sanctity, such as temples, need their thresholds protected even more. This division is the defining belief of animism; indeed it still has its echoes in the modern psyche.

One of the clearest statements of the necessity to protect the fragile transition between safe and unsafe worlds is found today among the Akha, Tibeto-Burman hill-tribes found widely dispersed along the borders of Yunan, Vietnam, Laos, Thailand and Burma. They are subsistence farmers whose main crop is cotton, and favourite food is dog. Primarily ancestor worshippers, the Akha also pay a great deal of attention to numerous unseen spirit forces (*neh*) that lurk in the jungle at the edge of their villages. These spirits are manifested in trees, rocks and streams, as well as termite hills and swamps; especially feared are the spirits of children who died before being named, or those of women who died in childbirth.

Originally, so Akha belief goes, humans and spirits lived together in paradisaical harmony, but greed for each others' property led to mutual hostility, and now the two realms must be clearly fenced off from each other by 'village gates' (*law kah*) at the upper and lower end of each settlement. Each time a person returns to the village they pass through one of these gates as a way of decontaminating themselves from outside influences, and any defilement of this highly sacred threshold is punished by a fine.

The gates are simple. Two wooden posts are flanked by roughly carved wooden figurines of a man and a woman (*tha pa mha*), sexual totems to ensure the continuity of life in the village, and bamboo charms (*da leh*) to ward off evil influences. The posts are surmounted by a crossbar hung with cuttings of bamboo and wooden replicas of birds and animals. There are also wooden weapons – which may be knives, spears, guns or crossbows, and since the days of American involvement in Vietnam, even planes and helicopters!

Each year the spirit gates are renewed to ensure their efficacy, a not uncommon ritual in the maintenance of sacred shrines. Young village men cut timber posts that are set up just beyond the previous years gate, creating an eerie avenue of gateways that gradually decompose with the passage of time.

LEFT Totem figure at a spirit gate, guarding the entrance to the village of Maw La Akha, Chiangrai, north Thailand.

Immortal Ancestors
Tangyue Memorial Arches, China

THERE IS NO DEATH, only a change of worlds. Our gross reality of embodied existence is only one of many, and is subject to constant and subtle influences from a variety of discarnate beings – spirits, ancestors, gods – of which most people are quite unconscious.

In China, both ancestors and gods were seen as part of a vast celestial bureaucracy, strictly organized as a centralized hierarchy very similar to the imperial civil service that governed the country. These ethereal mandarins keep a beady eye on the human realm, and contribute to the great importance the Chinese have always placed on family, dynastic and historical continuity.

These concerns have shaped Chinese ritual architecture throughout the centuries. A fine example can be seen in Anhui province, an area about 250 miles south-west of Shanghai, not far south of Huang Shan, the Yellow Mountain, traditionally an abode of the ancestors. A prosperous mercantile community flourished here, specializing in selling salt and the best calligraphic ink in the country. During the late Ming [A.D. 1368–1644] and Ching [A.D. 1644–1911] dynasties, its members built many splendid town houses with enclosed ornamental gardens, good examples of which can still be seen in the towns of Shexian and Yixian. The most prominent and competitive of the merchants strove to outdo each other by erecting family memorial arches (*paifang*), the best preserved of which are in the village of Tangyue.

Here, six of these monumental trabeated arches stand starkly in a line in the middle of flat fields, as if temporarily pausing in mid-stride on an infinitely long journey. They served as historical markers of an earthly existence that even their proud builders must sometimes have felt was insignificant against the surrounding vastness. Perhaps because of this, the arches were also to be seen as a tribute to all those departed ancestors who had passed this way before, and on whose shoulders each new generation stands.

'Men go out of life and enter into death...

He who may die but not perish has longevity.'

TAO TE CHING

LEFT The monumental forms of the Seven Memorial Arches of Tangyue village, Anhui province, Ming and Ching dynasties.

Imperial Tombs of the Perfume River, Vietnam

SET BESIDE THE PERFUME RIVER, in the thin strip of land that forms the heart of Vietnam, Hué became the imperial capital of the Nguyen lords of central Vietnam at the beginning of the seventeenth century. Modelled on the Chinese imperial capital of Peking, the walled city provided not only physical security in a land of chronic civil war, but the symbolic grandeur and introverted mystery appropriate to the court of semi-divine rulers. Vietnamese kings were traditionally buried in ancestral tomb complexes in their native village, but the Nguyen chose a grander type of

ABOVE AND OPPOSITE
Light filters through multi-coloured glass windows and doors into the wooden interior of the Ngung Hy Temple, in the royal tomb complex of Dong Khanh, Hué.

immortality, and established a divine necropolis a few kilometres to the west of their great capital, scattered over the hillsides that rise gently up from the banks of the Perfume River. In all, seven royal tombs and six pagodas form an atmospheric group here that well illustrates how the Vietnamese adapted well-tried Chinese architectural influences to create a distinctive style of their own.

The tombs (*lang*) are laid out in conformity with the Chinese desire to replicate earthly life after death. Each is essentially an introverted and miniaturized palace with three areas of increasing privacy. First comes a large brick-paved courtyard (*bia dinh*) containing a pavilion with marble or stone steles proclaiming the worth of the departed, and a 'spirit way' of numerous stone figures: attendants, courtiers, mandarin civil servants, soldiers, animals. Such retinues serve to ward off negative spirits, but they are also eerie reminders of the Chinese custom, prevalent up to at least 1000 B.C., whereby almost the entire court entered the Emperor's grave and was slaughtered, so he could be accompanied by his familiar entourage on his journey to the next life. Beyond the *bia dinh* courtyard comes the second area, the royal temple (*tam dien*), where the emperor and his queens were worshipped and their belongings displayed, and finally there is the hidden mausoleum (*bao thanh*), impenetrable behind high walls.

Tu Duc [1847–88], the fourth Nguyen Emperor, began the construction of his own tomb, Lang Tu Duc, in 1864. He loved to spend his time here, quietly reading and writing poetry, painting, fishing and contemplating the miniaturized paradise he had created. Indeed, he adopted the way of life idealized by both mystical Taoism and practical Confucianism, withdrawn from the febrile activity and

corruption of courtly life and close to nature. Particularly charming is his favourite lakeside Xung Khiem Pavilion, 'the modest abode', built in 1865, where he would sit and admire the creamy lotuses and water-lilies. They bloomed in the spring; Tu Duc, childless despite a harem of a hundred concubines, cuts an autumnal and rather melancholy figure, endearingly aware of his personal shortcomings and the fact that his reign

ABOVE AND RIGHT
The interior of the Ho Khiem Palace, tomb of Tu Duc, Hué; the bridge and garden from the Minh Lau Pavilion, tomb of Minh Mang, Hué.

stood teetering on the brink of yet another period of political and economic confusion.

Lang Tu Duc well illustrates the somewhat diffident character of Vietnamese architecture. Unlike the grand European house, the Vietnamese building never dominates its surroundings, but reveals itself only gradually, being partly hidden by specially planted shrubs and trees. Building and foliage are complementary parts of one whole in which inner and outer environments are linked. Corridors and passages in the house provide expansive vistas outwards while, reciprocally, trees help to compose and define courtyards and interior spaces by providing shade, protection and intimacy. Dominating verticals – banyans with their straggling aerial roots or tall, slim palms – are deliberately offset by subtle horizontal and miniaturized elements: low bushes, flowerbeds, pools, ceramic dishes for fish, lamps, fences, rockeries, bridges. Vietnamese architectural science places great importance on such harmony with natural surroundings, calling it *phong-thuy* ('wind-water-theory') after the Chinese *feng-shui*. Such harmony is not only an aesthetic ideal, but a paradigm of life lived aright, for it is the way of the sage, 'the superior man' who acts effortlessly in accord with Nature, at one with her rhythms and her laws.

Dong Khanh was an adopted son of Tu Duc, placed on the throne as a puppet ruler by the French colonial government. In his tomb, Lang Dong Khanh, the Ngung Hy Temple is particularly attractive, striking a judicious balance between Chinese-style bright polychrome decoration and a sense of uncluttered and airy space. While the pillared interior resembles an ordered and spacious forest clearing, in an outside courtyard a sacred tree and other overgrown shrines remind us of a less human, and thus more enduring, harmony.

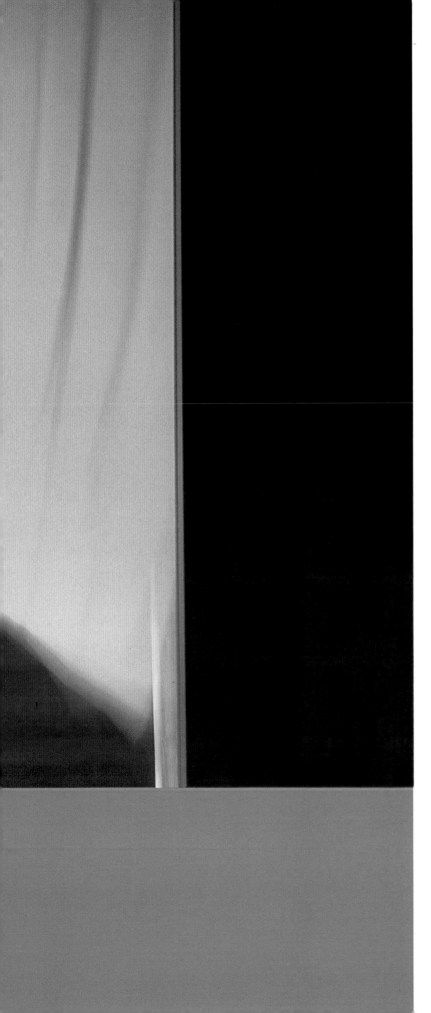

The Way of the Gods
Shinto

S hinto shrines have stood since the very dawn of recorded Japanese civilization, the Yamato conquests of around 600 B.C. In what has always been a small country of modest resources, these shrines (*jinja*) have the simplicity of nature itself. Wooden posts and beams support a gable roof – first doubtless thatch or bark, later shingle – to create a structure with the directness and economy that are the hallmarks of the Japanese classical aesthetic. Internally, the sanctuary is divided by an axial pillar into two equal chambers; indeed the building is almost the archetypal sacred tree extended in space, being made wholly of natural products – timber, bark, vines, bamboo and straw. The shrines are built from untreated and unpainted *hinoki*, a sacred Japanese cypress, grown in a special state forest far to the north, an area of mythical remoteness, redolent with spirituality in the Japanese psyche. Despite the strict axiality of their overall plan, these complexes evince above all harmony with the world of nature into which mankind has intruded as little as possible.

A unique feature of many Shinto shrines is their regular rebuilding. This practice, known as *sengu* ('the removal of the shrines'), takes place every twenty years as it has done for the last thirteen centuries. The last *sengu* at Ise-jingu took place in 1993; with the accompanying ceremony of Jingu Shikinen Sengu the deities were invited to move from the old to the new buildings. Their clothing and accoutrements, together with all the items used in their propitiatory rituals, are also renewed each 'generation'. Even in contemporary rebuilding, decoration is minimal – perhaps some curving of line and tasteful gilding of surface – resulting in an austerity that is in striking contrast to much Eastern architecture.

LEFT A rare glimpse of the lifting of the curtain, stirred by the 'divine wind' (*kamikaze*), at the shrine of Toyoukedai Jingu Shogu, Japan.

The Way of the Gods: *Miyajima, Japan*

IN THE SANCTUARY, the threshold is always crucial. It marks, protects and sanctifies the delicate transition from the profane outer world of change and death to the pure inner world where eternity is made manifest. Under the watchful eye of its guardians, the threshold invites us to abandon our habitual selves and step into the possibility of redemption and renewal; it is a boundary that promises the boundless.

The purest example of this ritual separation is the *torii* ('spirit perch') that fronts Japan's Shinto shrines. Soaring, stark and unadorned, these trabeated archways resemble a character of calligraphic script, elegant in their linear

ABOVE AND RIGHT
The Itsukushima-jinja shrine, Japan, and the 'floating Torii' at high tide.

simplicity, yet full of meaning. Originally ancient gateways, *torii* became limited to Shinto sanctuaries and other places of exceptional importance, and are traditionally made of plain wood, often painted vermilion. The pilgrim is purified by passing through them and is thus fit to proceed along the sacred path (*sando*), often lined by stone lanterns, that leads to the shrine itself. *Torii* are often found in the complexes of Buddhist temples, guarding a shrine of the local *kami* who is quite at home with the later religion. Shinto is a way that worships the spirits of nature, but its shrines are not found only in rural Japan; the flat roof of many an office block in the buzzing Ginza area of downtown Tokyo is graced by these elegantly minimalist structures. While some shrines have one or more, others contain veritable forests of *torii*; the Fushimi Inari shrine, for example, covers a whole mountain area in southern Kyoto with several thousand *torii* that have been presented as votive offerings by the faithful. And the numbers of worshippers served by a single *torii* may also be huge; of the 80 million Japanese reckoned to perform the *hatsumode* – the New Year visit to the shrine to pray for the gods' blessings – well over four million pilgrims pass through the massive *torii* fronting what is one of the most important Shinto sanctuaries, the Meiji in central Tokyo.

But of all *torii*, the most famous is the one that rises from the sea at Miyajima, 'the Island of Shrines', a few kilometres south of Hiroshima in south-west Honshu. Its proximity to the site of the atomic holocaust adds poignancy to the fact that this emblematic structure is Japan's greatest cultural icon, a symbol of the country to foreigners and natives alike. At high tide the blood-red arch rises from the rippling mirror of the Inland Sea; at low tide its form is shattered into a hundred

shards – miniature reflections in the puddles that dot the flat sandy shore.

At this stark crimson barrier the profane everyday world is dramatically forbidden entrance to the sanctity of the Itsukushima ('Strict Island') shrine, where the unstained purity of the eternal present is kept lively by the sonorous chanting of the monks. Itsukushima is well named. As the world of the spirit knows no time, so no birth and no death, the extreme markers of our brief passage on earth have been allowed on its sacred soil since recorded memory.

ABOVE AND RIGHT
The open-sided walkways of the Itsukushima shrine cross the shallow inlet on Miyajima island on stilts.

The Way of the Gods: *Ise-jingu, Japan*

THE HOLIEST SANCTUARY (*JINGU*) in Japan is at Ise, on the Shima peninsular in southern Honshu. This is the Grand Shrine, the supreme temple of Shinto, 'Way of the Gods', the islands' indigenous religion which worships many categories of spirit (*kami*), including the deities of nature and the ancestors. Historical evidence states that the inner shrine – *Naiku* – goes back to the 4th century A.D., and that the outer shrine – *Geku* – is perhaps a hundred years later, but in fact there have been centres of worship on this spot since time immemorial. Here, at the heart of the most westernized Asian nation, these simple wooden buildings preserve, unadulterated into modern times, a pure example of the classical animistic world-view. Ise is nothing less than the supreme embodiment of the Japanese soul.

In the second half of the 3rd century the shrine of Amaterasu, the Great Sun Goddess, was moved to Ise and she is the

ABOVE AND OPPOSITE
A cloth strip (*sakaki*) tied to a branch in the auxiliary sanctuary; a priest crosses its purifying moat.

main deity venerated in the inner shrine here. Traditionally the Emperor's daughter was her High Priestess (*saishu*), an office that still exists. The central shrine contains Amaterasu's mirror, one of the three sacred objects given to her great grandson Jimmu, the mythical First Emperor, as a token of the right of the Yamato imperial family to rule the world, which to them meant Japan. Through this mirror the royal family were believed symbolically to reflect and radiate the celestial solar energy; their dynasty only renounced its claims to divinity after Japan's defeat in the Second World War. The eastern shrine, aligned with the sun's rising, is the Sanctuary of the *Kami*, sacred to all the *kami* of heaven and earth, while the western, aligned with its setting, is the Sanctuary of Ancestral Spirits, that is, those of former Emperors. Worship here is an expression of devotion not only to the Sun Goddess, but to all that is most valued in the culture, history and racial consciousness of the Japanese people.

Another major *kami* occupies the *Geku*: Toyouke no Omikami, the Goddess of Agriculture and Food. Her shrine, established here in A.D. 478, is set in a tranquil grove of cryptomeria pine and cypress and surrounded by sacred paddy fields whose rice is used in ritual offerings to the goddess. The *Geku* also has the essential form of the very earliest shrines, a form frozen by religious conservatism. Such simple buildings were the seed of the great Japanese palaces of later times; indeed the words 'shrine' and 'palace' were for centuries virtually interchangeable in Japanese architectural vocabulary. The Ise shrines are stellar examples of the style known as *shinmei* ('divine brightness'), in which, in conformity with the general practice in the Far East, the entrance is in one of the long sides of a rectangular thatched building instead of in the gable

end. This form is still seen in the bamboo and straw shelters, set up alongside paddy fields all over Japan each autumn, the time all the *kami* in the land gather together. Tellingly, the vernacular name for these temporary structures translates as 'palace for the gods of Heaven and Earth'. Indeed, Shinto shrines always look somehow displaced in cities.

When Buddhism came to Japan from Korea, around A.D. 577, it was initially opposed by warring factions at the Imperial Court. Outbreaks of plague were attributed to the wrath of the traditional gods at having their primacy challenged by the new faith. But the newcomer that was to transform Japan persisted, and the architectural ideas it brought – essentially sophisticated Chinese building techniques transplanted and modified somewhat by Korean tastes – was the Chrysanthemum Throne's first real introduction to monumental architecture and the beginning of Japan's architectural history.

As the seat of Amaterasu, major lineage holder of Shinto shrines and preserver of traditional ways, Ise has always been Japan's pre-eminent site of pilgrimage. Purified by the sacred stream that protects the *Naiku*, several million would cross its wooden bridge during the periodic *okage mairi* pilgrimages. This importance dates particularly from the 13th century when the hereditary priests of the *Geku*, members of the Watarai family, made great efforts to promote Ise as a Shinto shrine to combat the influence of Buddhism. In time, though, it became the familiar story of indigenous gods blending seamlessly with an incoming religion. Most Japanese today barely differentiate between *kami* and Buddhas; indeed the inclusive term *shinbutsu*, made up of the ideograms for *kami* and *butsu* (Buddha), is used to signify both forms of wish-fulfilling deity.

LEFT AND ABOVE
A procession of priests
arriving at the main
sanctuary, Ise-jingu,
carrying a Shinto ark
(*karahitsu*); a female
attendant cleans the
entrance to Kaguradon,
Hall of Sacred Music
and Dance; the central
buildings of the inner
sanctuary.

ABOVE AND OPPOSITE Icons
of Hinduism at Varanasi:
Shiva's bull Nandi and the
footprints of Vishnu.

THE MOTHER

THE WEST CALLS IT HINDUISM, but to the Indians it is *Sanatana Dharma,* 'The Eternal Law': a total way of life, guiding the evolution of its adherents from the moment of conception to the cremation pyre, and beyond. With no historical founder, no central organization and no head of the church, this extraordinarily rich mixture of belief and practice, accumulated in the sub-continent over five thousand years or more, covers a spectrum stretching from primitive rites of archaic magic and animal sacrifice to the subtlest philosophy and world-view the human mind has ever conceived.

To the Hindu the entire universe is permeated by one Divine Consciousness (*brahman*). The source of all life, *brahman* is an impersonal transcendental field, inaccessible to direct worship, yet manifesting itself as the endlessly diverse world. Linking this abstract reality with the concrete day-to-day world are the subtle levels of life, the invisible realms that form the unconscious springs of our thought and action. These hidden energies are personified in the vast and complicated Hindu pantheon – not only the major and minor deities, but a whole host of celestial and infernal creatures. Viewed aright, Hinduism is as

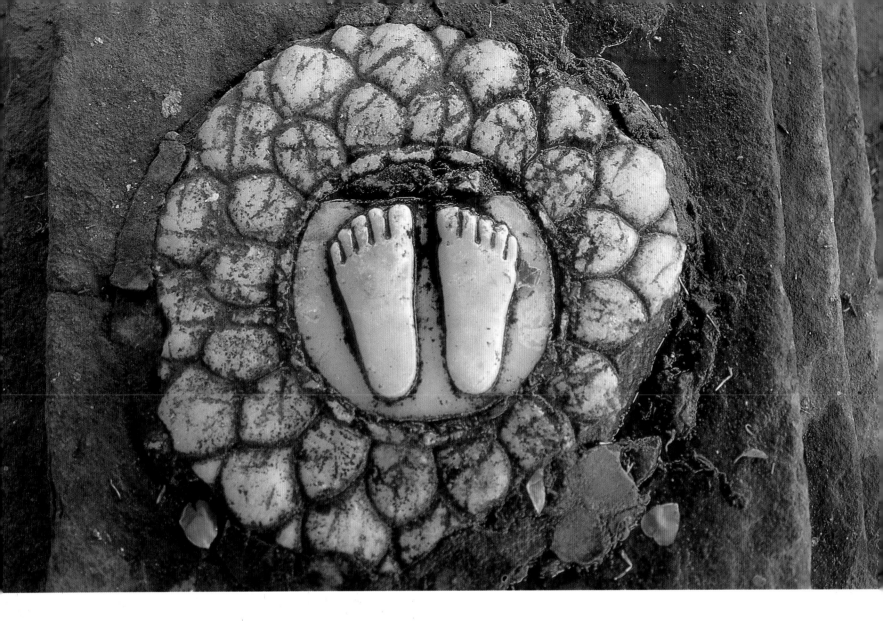

RELIGION OF ASIA
Hinduism and its Influence

monotheistic as the Semitic faiths, for all the deities are but aspects of the one *brahman*, facets of the one jewel. While popular Hinduism is concerned with invoking and worshipping these deities to gain their favour in daily life, its esoteric side, which includes the non-denominational teachings of *yoga*, is concerned with refining and developing the ability to experience the one *brahman* within all things: Enlightenment. Hindus believe that there are as many ways to the Divine as there are seekers of it. Indeed, it was by constantly incorporating the racial and cultural variety of a land-mass as large and diverse as Europe,

that the faith managed to survive and prosper. This flexibility resulted in an extraordinary pluralism. In the context of this book, it allows Jainism and Sikhism, though certainly venerable religions in their own right, to be included as examples of the many facets of the pan-Indian phenomenon that is *Sanatana Dharma*. Popular Hinduism never really spread widely outside the land of its origin, but because its priestly caste, the *brahmins*, were renowned throughout the ancient world for their proficiency in all branches of learning and culture, they gave Hinduism a wider influence, so distinctive in the sites described here.

Varanasi, North India
Holy Mother Ganges

WHICHEVER OF ITS NAMES YOU USE – Varanasi, Benares or Kashi – this is the oldest centre of pilgrimage and the most extraordinary city in the world. According to legend, Kashi, 'City of Light', was the first of all cities, built by the first king in a forest carpeted with sacred *kusha* grass. Long before the days of Babylon, Solomon's Temple or the glories of Nebuchadnezzar, Kashi was already a thriving centre of civilization, a place of priestly expertise which the great god Shiva, Lord of Transformation, had chosen to make his earthly home. The entire city, with its two thousand temples, is dedicated to him, and it is the holiest place on earth for the Hindu. To end one's life here is to be assured of not just a place in heaven or a favourable rebirth, but total liberation from *samsara* – the eternal round of birth and death.

All the impressions of India are concentrated here in a sensual maelstrom, and all her seeming contradictions, for Varanasi is the quintessence of Hinduism. The place can be quite a test for the Western visitor, for nowhere else is India so radically different from what he is used to. For those to whom plenty is assured, death disguised, and religion little more than a corporate consolation, Varanasi can be overwhelming. Being imperiously nudged out of the way by a sacred cow may be just tolerable, but seeing a corpse crackle as it is devoured by the hungry flames may be too much reality to take. But Varanasi amply rewards those who can stay with her and her powerful energies, for once you have been here, your life will never be the same.

Varanasi is what she is because of where she is: on the banks of the holy Ganges. Personified as the mighty goddess Ganga, she first descended from heaven with such power that Shiva had to filter her mighty flow through his matted locks. Now, this flat, calm stretch of

'Are there not many holy places on this earth? Yet which of them would equal in the balance one speck of Kashi's dust? Are there not many rivers running to the sea? Yet which of them is like the River of Heaven in Kashi?'

KASHI KHANDA

OPPOSITE AND THIS PAGE
Scenes from a holy city: bodies await cremation at Manikarnika Ghat; a bridegroom leads his bride after a blessing by waterside priests.

Holy Mother Ganges

ABOVE AND OPPOSITE
Morning mists over
the Ganges at Varanasi;
bathers seek the holy
water by the tower
of Manikarnika Ghat;
washing clothes at
Balaji Ghat.

water that seems to go on for ever is the pulsing artery through which the life blood of Hinduism flows. Starting as a crystal clear rivulet at the 'Cow's Mouth' of Gangotri in the high Himalayas, she widens and lengthens over 1,250 miles, sanctifying site after site, to end by exploding into the profusion of waters that empty joyously into the Bay of Bengal. She is the Hindu's link to the pure vastness of the Himalayas, where only the saints and the gods can dwell, and as 'Mother Ganges' she is the bringer of life to the north Indian plains.

The city's divine pre-eminence has not spared Varanasi from the vicissitudes of history. It remained under Hindu rule until the twelfth century, when, as the religious capital of the north, it suffered terribly at the hands of Islam. In the seventeenth century, the Mughal emperor Shah Jehan, builder of the Taj Mahal, had seventy-six temples destroyed here, and his son Auranzeb continued the persecution, razing temples and impoverishing Hindu cultural institutions. The year 1669 was perhaps the blackest – two of the city's most sacred shrines, the temple of Bindu Madhava dedicated to Lord Vishnu, and the Shiva Vishvanatha temple were destroyed and, to compound the insult, mosques built in their place. But nothing drives humanity into the arms of God as swiftly as suffering; rebuilt, the Shiva Vishvanatha Temple, popularly known as the Golden Temple due to its gold-plated dome, flourishes once more as the sacred centre of the city, protected by five concentric rings of sanctity, marked out by shrines, that mimic the five subtle 'bodies' enveloping the human soul.

Following the principles of sacred architecture, Varanasi is built only on the west bank of the river, the east bank left completely unobstructed to allow the full enlivening force of the new day to irradiate the city. The old quarter is a labyrinth of unmarked lanes and alleys, wide enough only for pedestrians and animals, that snake their way down to the waterfront steps (*ghats*). Here the whole panoply of Hinduism unfolds each morning as pilgrims and locals come to the river bank to pray, meditate and perform their early morning rituals. An important one is *surya darshana*, which honours the sun as the mighty being Surya, endlessly generous source of light, intelligence, and life. Cooling water is offered and trickled down in front of the eyes, acting as a shield through which the intense light enlivens the hypothalamus and whole nervous system.

The *ghats* are also the place to meet, gossip, do ones's washing, and seek out the priests who sit under tattered parasols waiting to perform the manifold rituals that punctuate the Hindu calendar. Varanasi is preeminently a priestly city, with all the strengths and weaknesses that implies. Traditionally a great centre of Sanskrit learning and sacred expertise, it is equally famed for its silk, music, love of pleasure and crazy humour fuelled, no doubt, by the hashish freely available here.

Life, and her silent sister death, go on day after day here, as they have done since time immemorial. Each morning and evening thanks for the gift of life are offered on behalf of the whole city in the Mother Ganga temple on Dasashvamedha *ghat*, while further upriver, on the cremation ground of Manikarnika Ghat, the funeral pyres never rest. With all her contradictions, Varanasi is living proof that when a place is held to be holy for sufficiently long, the Divine takes up residence there.

LEFT AND THIS PAGE
Treading the path of pilgrimage: a *sadhu* on the steps of Lal Ghat; another climbs the steps of Kedar Ghat, while another meditates, surrounded by his worldly possessions.

ABOVE AND RIGHT
Greeting the rising
sun from the Ghats;
worshippers first bathe,
then salute the sun
with water, and finally
sit in morning
meditation – all against
the backdrop of the
waterfront.

Pashupatinath, Nepal
Shiva, Lord of All Creatures

SOME THREE MILES EAST of Kathmandu stands the holiest temple in Nepal, dedicated to the mighty god Shiva in his benign form as Pashupatinath: 'Lord of all Creatures'. The present form of the complex, the square two-roofed Newar design, dates from only 1696; but for over a thousand years this has been the royal temple – and the fine gilt and silverwork attests to continued patronage. As one of the four holiest Shiva temples, Pashupatinath draws devotees from all over Hindu Asia; it is also deemed one of the twenty-four Tantric power places of the sub-continent.

Though the place may initially seem unremarkable aesthetically, it radiates an extraordinarily charged atmosphere, reminding us that the prime function of such a site is not to please the eye, but to radiate the power of the primal energies which the Hindu deities embody. Entrance to the temple is forbidden to non-Hindus; through the gates one can catch a tantalizing glimpse of a huge gilded bull. This is Nandi ('The Joyous') who represents nature's elemental energy. The inner shrine houses a *chaturmukhalinga*, a *lingam* carved with four faces looking to the cardinal points. It is covered by a silver sheath topped by the crown of Bhairava, the fierce form of Shiva, worshipped throughout the kingdom. Hinduism and Buddhism are uniquely intertwined in Nepal; Buddhists worship this *lingam* as a form of their deity Avalokiteshvara, embodiment of compassion, and are permitted to crown it once a year as a celestial being, a *bodhisattva*.

Pashupatinath stands on the the banks of the holy Bagmati river, overlooking Arya *ghat* where the royal family and high castes are cremated. The whole area has always been the territory of the *sadhu*, the wandering mendicant who, having renounced all social ties and obligations, acts out the untamed side of Hindu spirituality. The wooded hillocks here are pitted with their caves. One group, the *Aghoris* ('the Fearless'), still practise their meditations at the cremation grounds on the river bank and are said to indulge in ritual cannibalism. The great saint Adi Shankara visited Pashupatinath in the 9th century A.D. to re-establish the purity of Shiva worship, and since the 15th century the temple has been run by an hereditary succession of orthodox South Indian *brahmins*, though there are still many small Tantric temples and shrines outside the main complex, along with some extraordinarily beautiful, and sadly neglected, sculptures dating from the Licchavi period (7th century A.D.), the golden age of Nepalese art.

Pashupatinath is at its wildest at Mahashivaratri, 'the Night of Shiva', each February-March full moon, when tens of thousands of wandering *sadhus* congregate here from all corners of the subcontinent. Long hair and beards unkempt and matted with sacred cow-dung, they smear their bodies a spectral grey with ash from funeral pyres, and smoke hashish as a ritual stimulant to aid their devotions. Some travel alone, others on horseback or in quasi-military cadres. Fiercest of all are the naked *nagas*, traditionally first in the pecking order, who are armed with spears, daggers, swords or muskets. Necks strung with beads and amulets, all carry their few possessions: a water pot, a blanket and the trident (*trishula*) that signifies their lord Shiva. This motley caravan defies easy judgement: some may be work-shy charlatans or fugitives from the mother-in-law or the police, others ascetics of genuine spiritual attainment. For the duration of Mahashivaratri they are all provided with accommodation in pilgrim rest-houses, one meal a day and firewood, by order of the king.

THIS PAGE AND OPPOSITE
Red-dressed women for the Teej festival; erotic pillar carvings; a devotee massages a *sadhu*.

Nilakantha, Nepal
The Lord of Creation Sleeps

EACH MORNING, as the sun rises over the Kathmandu Valley, its rays fall gently on an adamantine figure lying on a bed formed by the twisting coils of a giant serpent. To the Buddhists this sleeping colossus suspended in the midst of his sacred pool is a form of Avalokiteshvara, Deity of Universal Compassion, and to the followers of Shiva he is Nilakantha, 'the Blue-Throated One', so-called because he swallowed the poison of mortality at the dawn of time. But to most he is the great Lord Vishnu, in his form as Narayana, 'He who Lies on the Waters'. In this form Vishnu, personification of the never-ending process of cosmic evolution, is resting, and the febrile activity of the material universe has come to a temporary halt. While he sleeps, everything returns to the unmanifest state; when he starts to dream, the next cosmic cycle (*yuga*), reckoned to last almost half a million years, will begin. Thus life continues, in alternating cycles of the great god's sleep and dream, throughout all eternity.

As the sun climbs higher in the sky, specially qualified *brahmin* priests, whose fathers and grandfathers before them have had the same responsibility since A.D. 641, serve the image: cleaning it, lustrating it with holy water and perfume, burning incense and waving fans over it, painting its face and body with elaborate decorative marks in yellow, red and white and bedecking it with garlands of marigold and jasmine. They lie brilliant against the blackly oiled basalt. All the while the priests chant the Sanskrit verses of the *Vishnusahasranama*, 'The thousand names of the All-Pervading One'. But despite all this attention (or perhaps because he likes it), Narayana sleeps peacefully on.

Vishnu Narayana is never visited by a member of the Nepalese royal family. In the mid 17th century, King Pratap Malla had a dream in which he was told by the god that if he or any of his successors approached the shrine, they would forfeit their life. Thus were the Kings of the Valley, themselves incarnations of Narayana, protected from being destroyed by gazing on the image of their own divine nature.

One can only marvel at the skill with which Hindu sculptors express the abstract insights of their faith in concrete form. Narayana's four hands – the upper pair hold a sun-disk and a mace, the lower a seed and a conch – symbolize the four cardinal directions, and the four great *yugas*, from the perfect Golden Age to the present degenerate Kali Age, through which each cycle of manifestation passes. The sun is the intelligent source of all light and life in our solar system, while the mace repesents the regal authority and order of the Natural Law through which Vishnu governs the evolving universe. His lower hands connect macrocosm to microcosm, deity to devotee. The seed, moved to sprout by its own hidden energy, shows the hidden potential of divinity in each one of us, while the conch alludes to the power of sound, through which, in chanting and meditation on sacred mantras, we activate this seed and realize our true nature, the boundless light within.

'Thou art the First of Gods, the Primal Person,
the supreme resting place of the world.
Thou art the knower and that which is to be known,
and the supreme goal.
And by Thee this universe is pervaded,
O Thou of infinite form!'

BHAGAVAD GITA

LEFT *Brahmin* priests cleanse the statue of Nilakantha, Lord Vishnu on a bed of serpent coils, Buranilkantha in the Kathmandu valley.

Tiruvannamalai, South India
The Hill of Light

IT IS SAID THERE WAS once a dispute between the great gods Vishnu and Brahma as to whom was the mightier. Overhearing their quarrel the greatest of the trinity, Lord Shiva, seized the initiative and, turning himself into an infinite column of fire, declared that whoever found the end of the column would win the argument. Vishnu immediately took the form of a boar and began burrowing down into the earth, while Brahma became a bird and flew far into the skies. Much later, Vishnu was the first to return. He humbly admitted his defeat: the column had no end. When Brahma returned, however, he at first tried to claim that he had reached the summit. His lie exposed, he was condemned to forfeit the right to public worship, and to this day there are only a couple of active temples dedicated to him in the entire subcontinent, while those of Shiva and Vishnu are without number. At the end of the epic contest, the infinite fiery *lingam* took solid form and became what is now known as Arunachala, the 'Hill of Light' that overlooks the small south Indian town of Tiruvannamalai. It is one of the most extraordinary places on earth.

Shiva's cosmic apparition is commemorated each year on the night of the tenth lunar day of the month of Karttika (October–November). A huge bonfire is lit on the summit of the hill; it burns for days and is visible for miles around as the flaming emblem of the Lord of Transformation. Thousands of pilgrims circumambulate the hill, prostrating themselves and chanting. For the rest of the year, worship centres on the man-made form of the fiery *lingam* that is enshrined in the holy of holies of the town's Arunachaleshvara temple. This is the *jyoti lingam* ('lingam of light'), one of five uniquely important *lingams* that embody the five great elements – earth, water, fire, air and space – from which the universe is made. Each of these images must be under regular worship if the coherence of the universe is to be maintained. While the Arunachaleshvara *lingam*, embodying the element fire, is being worshipped, elsewhere in India the other elements are being held in their place by similar devotions.

As befits its importance, the Arunachaleshvara is the largest Shiva temple in South India and a magnificent complex, composed of three concentric enclosures around spacious courtyards that house in addition to the main temple a variety of buildings – the immense thousand-pillar hall, numerous smaller shrines, tanks, and groves of graceful palm trees. Four enormous entrance gateways (*gopurams*) in the outer wall are aligned with the cardinal points, each other and the four smaller gates to the second enclosure, giving the whole structure a pleasing symmetry. Most spectacular of the outer *gopurams* is the eastern one. Towering 66 metres over the main entrance, it rises as a soaring pyramid of ten diminishing brick and stucco registers set on a massive granite base profusely carved with the gods and goddesses. In front of this imposing entrance a large and colourful bazaar caters busily to the needs of the many pilgrims who visit.

'Oh Arunachala, you root out the ego of those who meditate on you at the heart.'

BHAGAVAN SHRI RAMANA MAHARSHI

THIS PAGE AND OPPOSITE
Pilgrims gather at
the Arunachaleshvara
temple to receive
blessings.

The temple of
Arunachaleshvara,
viewed from the hill-
dwelling of a *sadhu*;
the eastern *gopuram* of
the temple dominates
the whole complex
and surrounding plain.

The Hill of Light

In September 1896 another chapter in the story of Arunachala began. An uneducated youth arrived here and never left, yet he was to become famous the world over as Ramana Maharshi, one of the purest examples of the enlightened being or liberated soul (*jivanmukti*) ever known. Born in 1879, the son of a pious *brahmin* family, Ramana underwent a spontaneous enlightenment at the age of sixteen. Leaving his native Madurai with only three rupees for the train fare, he arrived at Arunachala, called by some power. He spent his first three years there in absolute silence, living first in the temple, and then retiring to caves on the hill. Little by little people gathered around him to receive his *darshan* and he began to teach. The essence of his message was that each and every one of us is the immortal Divine if we can only recognize It as our own infinite and eternal Self. He conveyed this highest of spiritual truths, known as *Advaita Vedanta*, by answering devotees' questions in a direct, simple manner spiced with a gentle humour, and by the transforming power of the silence he radiated. He also composed numerous devotional songs and poems, many of them directed to Arunachala as a living form of Shiva himself.

Ramana never left his beloved hill, but gradually word of him spread far and wide. Spiritual seekers from all over the world, rich and poor, high and low, made the often arduous journey here. He received them all with perfect equality and unfailing courtesy; none went away untouched. In time he became part of the very folklore of the sub-continent, its ancient ideal of Enlightenment lived out in our time. Modern media spread his fame: Cartier-Bresson's poignant photographs of the sage at the end of his life in 1950 illuminate what is the most evocative of Indian portfolios.

These days the *ashram* Ramana established at the foot of the hill is buzzing with activity. Many of its visitors are Westerners; some of them will have been drawn here by the pellucid compassion of his gaze, arresting even in photographs, others may have logged on to the *ashram's* website. Yet despite trappings of modernity and the danger of becoming a spiritual tourist attraction, this place still has a timeless atmosphere for those who can allow the mind to settle. To do the ritual walk around the hill in the early morning is to step out of time and imbibe the extraordinary peace and silence it seems to exude. There is something of eternity here and an exemplary combination of the three great keynotes of Indian spirituality here: a locus of Divine power, a temple which focuses that power, and a saint who embodies and radiates it for the good of the world.

ABOVE AND RIGHT
A temple elephant blesses a pilgrim; worshippers gather before a statue of Nandi, Shiva's bull, outside the temple.

Kanchipuram, South India
City of Sages

SOARING HIGH ABOVE the glittering emerald paddy fields where white eagrets stalk fastidiously, their long necks craned for fish and frogs, are the towers. Massive truncated pyramids, they radiate power, for these imperious structures are the entry portals (*gopurams*) of a south Indian temple. They simultaneously proclaim the presence of the deity whose shrine they guard, and summon the traveller, as they have done for hundreds of years, to partake of their charge's blessing. Part defence, part sheer aspiration, the *gopuram* is as much a feature of this part of the sub-continent as the ubiquitous coconut palm, or the patient wooden bullock carts, wheels splayed out at fantastic angles, that creak and sway in rural unconcern along the dappled roads.

Long before you reach Kanchipuram, Tamil Nadu's most sacred city and one of Mother India's seven *mokshapuris* ('cities of liberation'), you feel the excitement. For this town of temples – some say over a hundred – has been for millennia a meeting point of scholars and sages, priests and poets. As the spiritual capital of Tamil civilization, it is hymned as the heart of the original India, unpolluted by foreign influences and the degenerate ways of *Kali yuga*, the present age of darkness. Did not Lord Rama himself, on his way to rescue the kidnapped Sita from the clutches of the ten-headed demon Ravana,

have his mission blessed here? Did he not return to give thanks for his success, and stay long enough to initiate his loyal monkey-general Hanumanji in Kanchi's holy places? And didn't great saints like Adi Shankara, Agastya and Ramanuja choose to live here, and Kalidasa, the most celebrated of India's dramatists, and the famous historian Kautilya? Sanctified by the country's most illustrious hearts and minds, Kanchi is a stellar example of the city as energy converted into culture.

As the capital of a succession of mighty southern dynasties, Pallava (6th–9th centuries A.D.) Chola (9th–12th centuries) and Vijayanagar (15th–17th centuries), Kanchi enjoyed abundant royal patronage, materialized in exemplarily tolerant fashion in the city's three sacred zones: Shiva Kanchi, Vishnu Kanchi and Jaina Kanchi. Every so often attractive traditional houses with tiled roofs and leisurely verandahs supported by brightly painted wooden columns suddenly give way to the immense protective walls of a temple. Many are large composite complexes, added to by each new ruler. The Varadaraja, dedicated to Vishnu, has a thousand-pillar assembly hall (*mandapa*) superbly carved with lions and soldiers on horseback as reminders of the military prowess of its Vijayanagar builders.

At the other end of town stands the Ekambeshvara, dedicated to Shiva, its massive entrance *gopuram* a double series of granite walls

> *'Just as cakes become sweet when they are coated with sugar frosting,
> so do places in this world become holy and pure when a saint abides in them.'*
>
> PUJYAPADA, A JAIN SAINT

THIS PAGE AND OPPOSITE South Indian stone carving: images of Hanuman, the monkey god, (*opposite* and *far right*), Durga (*left*) and Lakshmi (*centre*).

supporting nine storeys of stuccoed brickwork, surmounted by a vaulted roof soaring 60 metres from the ground. The holy of holies contains an especially important *lingam*, the 'earth *lingam*', which, as one of the *panchbhutalingams* representing the five elements, needs to be regularly worshipped to keep the material world in balance. It is believed that Shiva married his consort here; at a great festival in the month of Chaitra (March/April) many couples emulate the gods and tie the knot in the *kalyan mandapa*.

In the middle of the town, behind red, gold and blue *gopurams* of a Disneyland brilliance, lies the Kamakshi Amman temple, dedicated to the goddess Kamakshi, 'Wanton-eyed', as protectress of the city. Depicted with a bow made of sugar cane from which she fires flower-tipped arrows of desire at her victims, the image was consecrated by the greatest of all Hindu teachers, Adi Shankara (9th century A.D.). Renouncing the world when he was nine, and dying when he was thirty-two, Shankara was sage, saint, poet, scholar and administrator. He reformed the organizational structure of Hinduism, returning it to its pure Vedic roots by founding ten orders of monks, and five principal monasteries overseen by a line of administrator-teachers called the Shankaracharyas.

The Kamakoti Peetham, an unremarkable pinkish building not far from the Kamakshi temple, is the seat of the southern Shankaracharya. The monastery is very busy in promoting educational and charitable projects and furthering the

RIGHT A fierce *yali* guards a shrine with a black basalt *yoni-lingam* in the Kailashanatha temple, dedicated to Shiva.

current renaissance of Tamil culture. Each day the Shankaracharya makes himself tirelessly available to a seemingly endless stream of pilgrims from all walks of life, listening to grievances, offering advice, giving blessings. Many of the visitors just stand watching him with rapt wordless attention, enjoying the *darshan*, ('sighting'), the process whereby some of a saint's bliss may seep into those in his presence by a kind of spiritual osmosis. The whole business is very moving; the monastery is charged with an extraordinary atmosphere of vibrant silence and there is a deep happiness in many of these faces.

ABOVE AND RIGHT
The temple of
Ekambareshvara:
the main tank and
thousand-pillar hall;
the pavilion with
elaborate carvings
stands opposite
the main *gopuram*,
where the deities rest
during temple
processions.

Tirumala, South India
Vishnu, Maintainer of the Cosmos

THE TEMPLE OF TIRUMALA has been active since the 9th century, but much of the elegant early architecture, dating mainly from the 15th and 16th centuries, has been obscured by modern additions to serve the ever increasing number of pilgrims. Once inside the complex many of these go straight to squatting lines of barbers who will shave their heads as a final purification; India's thriving wig industry derives largely from Tirumala. But before the *darshan* is vouchsafed these pilgrims face one further test. So great are the crowds that they will have to wait for up to twelve hours, shuffling along in interminable lines behind wire fences, sustained only by their chanting and their hopes, before being granted the briefest glimpse of their god.

He waits imperiously for them under a golden roofed shrine in the centre of the complex, Lord Venkateshvara – Lord Srinivasa as he is popularly known – a form of Vishnu, Preserver of the Cosmos. Everything about the figure radiates power. So garlanded is Lord Srinivasa that only his crowned black face and his feet are visible, and his eyes are permanently covered to save the world from being burnt up by the force of their gaze; it is believed he can grant any wish.

Tirumala is said to be the richest temple in the sub-continent. In a typical day ten thousand pilgrims come to pay their respects; in a typical year they will donate a fortune in notes and coins and over 350 kgs. of gold and silver to its treasury. Most of this goes to fund charitable hospitals, colleges and orphanages, and to provide free accommodation and food for the pilgrims. The *pujas* here can be enormous events, going on for hours. At the main annual festival no less than thirty-two types of flowers, weighing a total of 2450 kgs., are offered, and each day dozens of different dishes of cooked and uncooked food are placed at Lord Srinivasa's flower-decked feet.

To serve the demands of its incumbent deity, this pulsating citadel of the sacred employs almost 6000 souls, each according to his hereditary function. A strictly graded hierarchy is topped by those priests who have exclusive responsibility for feeding, dressing, cleaning and worshipping the main image and its many companions. Next come all those whose combined efforts provide the offerings that tempt the immaterial energy of the deity to descend into the image and thereby bless the community – cooks, suppliers of food, fruit, flowers, camphor and oil; workers in gold, silver and copper who make lamps, bells, trays, pots and bowls; carpenters, painters and makers of garlands, wicks and leaf platters; assorted temple musicians and dancers – the list goes on. Inevitably, a huge bureaucracy handles the day-to-day organization, including the accountants and clerks who tally up the vast static wealth heaped in the temple vaults, and the armed security staff who protect it. And last of all come the humble cleaners and sweepers. Such people traditionally occupy the lowest rung in the social order, yet to be even a cleaner in the service of Lord Srinivasa is a job many would covet, for who can predict which of his countless devotees he will deign to bless?

THIS PAGE AND OPPOSITE Scenes from the Tirumala temple, dedicated to Vishnu, at Tirupati: pilgrims gather to enter the holy of holies; the main *gopuram*; waiting for *darshan*; offerings of marigold and burning camphor.

Angkor Wat, Cambodia
Citadel of the God Kings

ONE MORNING IN 1860, a French naturalist called Henri Mouhot turned a corner on a forest path in the Cambodian jungles that lay about a hundred-and-fifty miles north-west of the present-day capital Phnom Penh. He halted in astonishment. Scarcely able to believe what he saw, he was faced with a vision of ghostly pyramidal stone towers, soaring weightlessly above a serpentine embrace of creepers, trees and undergrowth, that took his breath away. In his search for rare butterflies, Mouhot had stumbled upon the ruins of Angkor Wat, the royal temple-mausoleum of the god-king Suryavarman that had lain hidden for four centuries. The Khmers of Cambodia left the world no great inventions or systems of administration like those of China, and no sublime spiritual philosophies to compare with those of India, but they were unsurpassed builders, sculptors and decorators in stone, and this is why the temples of Angkor are among humanity's greatest treasures.

The first great ruler of the Khmers was Jayavarman II, who in about A.D. 800 established a kingdom, constitution and religion that were to last for over six hundred years. Raising his new capital in the region where Angkor now stands, Jayavarman summoned a *brahmin* priest and instructed him to perform a rare ceremony which would stabilize the new kingdom and break for ever its subservience to the powerful Saliendra empire in neighbouring Java. The priest surpassed expectations: he performed a ritual whereby Jayavarman experienced the universal consciousness, his body becoming the earthly vehicle of Lord Shiva himself. Henceforward the king was not just a representative of heaven on earth, but was actually a divine being, worthy not only of respect and obedience, but of worship. The supreme symbol of this apotheosis became the *lingam*, already familiar to the many Shiva worshippers throughout Greater India.

Thus was established the cult of Devaraja,'the god-king'. From Jayavarman onwards the Khmer kings were regarded as demi-gods, and many great complexes were constructed in their honour. The

'Then, all at once, I was suddenly transported from

barbarism to civilization, from profound darkness to light.'

HENRI MOUHOT, ON HIS FIRST SIGHTING OF ANGKOR WAT

OPPOSITE AND THIS PAGE
The sun sets over the crowning towers of Angkor, model of Mount Meru; carvings of celestial dancers (*apsaras*) grace the walls and galleries; carvings embellish the second terrace and the entrance galleries.

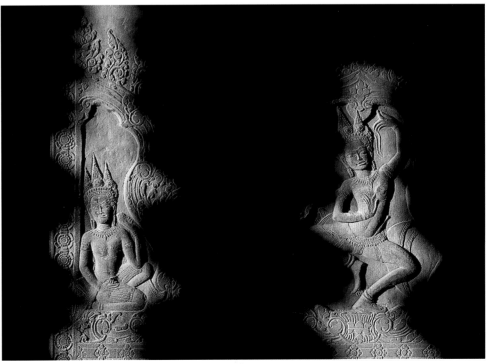

Citadel of the God Kings

ABOVE AND OPPOSITE
The statuary of
Angkor Wat is rich
and fabulous, as Henri
Mouhot discovered:
detail of a sinuous
apsara; a statue of
Vishnu, eight-armed
embodiment of cosmic
stability in the west
entrance gallery.

greatest of these is Angkor Wat, built in the first half of the 12th century by the Sun King Suryavarman II to be both a royal Vishnu temple and his own mausoleum. Angkor is the contemporary of some of the great European cathedrals – Notre-Dame de Paris and Chartres in France, Lincoln and Ely in England – but in size and grandeur of conception it outshines them all.

Over four-hundred-and-fifty Khmer monuments in Cambodia alone – and many others in Laos, Vietnam and Thailand – show the gradual evolution that culminated in the magnificence of this sacred citadel. The simple Khmer shrine, a single tower made of brick on a square plan with an entrance porch, expanded by stages to become a many-towered shrine set on imperious, terraced pyramids, while clusters of hitherto discrete structures became linked by a series of vaulted corridors and enclosed quadrangles to form one mighty complex.

While Angkor's lengthy approach is perfectly dramatized to strike awe into the visitor, its lingering majesty stems as much from the easeful reconciliation of complementary features. The huge spatial area is fleshed out with perfect proportion; decorative detail, itself offset by judicious use of unworked surfaces, is always within the context of an overall grandeur that borders on austerity. Heavy stone horizontals, walls, corbels and vaulting are always lightened and balanced by the insistent and graceful upward sweep of the towers. On closer inspection, the solid stone dissolves into the finest decoration, sometimes so faint as to be barely visible, elsewhere – especially where wind and rain have not penetrated – clearly etched. Particularly remarkable is the frieze that runs eight-feet-high round the lowest terrace. Here gods, goddesses, and

sensuous nymphs dance among serene ascetics, while animals and soldiers act out episodes from the *Ramayana* and *Mahabharata*. Suryavarman, the great incarnation and devotee of Vishnu, is shown alongside Rama, battling the ten-headed demon Ravanna, personification of evil. One would expect no less from a god-king of Angkor.

Viewed from the air, Angkor's geometrical design becomes clear. The jungle opens to reveal a square moat, its mile-long sides scintillating in the sun, crossed by a stone causeway leading to the main entrance. Following the laws of *sthapthya veda*, this imposing gateway, one of four aligned with the cardinal points, faces East to receive the rising sun. The gateway, set into a high wall fortified at each corner, leads in turn to an inner courtyard, vast enough to accommodate thousands, set with tanks of sacred water to reflect the sunlight, cool and purify the air and create an atmosphere of tranquillity. A second, lower wall, itself more than a mile in circumference, protects a further enclosure, from the centre of which rise, on a base of three tiered stages, the five majestic towers of the shrine itself. These are ordered on the classical Indian plan called *pancharatna* ('five jewels'): four towers at the mid points of the compass surround the higher central one, which rises here almost two hundred and twenty feet above the shining moat and water tanks, as the mighty Mount Meru rises from the Cosmic Ocean. The cosmic energy gathered by this mountain-antenna is radiated out through the four subsidiary towers and the four gateways. Thus was the whole of Suryavarman's kingdom aligned with the almighty governing forces of nature, thereby ensuring peace, prosperity and lasting happiness.

Chandi Sukuh and Chandi Ceto, Java

Sacred Sexuality

THE FORM IS ARCHETYPAL: a truncated pyramid which could be a Mayan temple, an Mesopotamian ziggurat, or a tribal meeting place from prehistoric Polynesia. But, in fact, we are in central Java, on the sacred slopes of Mount Lawu, long a site where ancestors gathered and kings were buried. In the first half of the 15th century, this pyramid, the temple we know as Chandi Sukuh, was built here, weaving a newer strand into the multi-hued tapestry that is Javanese culture. This was Hinduism, in particular its esoteric schools of *tantra* – that teach the secret, rapid path to Enlightenment. Both ancestor worship and *tantra* share a concern for liberation from all earthly bonds. A clue to their common purpose lies in the Javanese word for temple: *chandi*, a term derived from one of the names of Durga, the fearsome goddess of death, who is also one of the main tantric deities. Thus a *chandi* is a place which provides the correct setting for rites dealing with death and resurrection.

Even today, the place has a weird, primeval atmosphere. Three pyramidal gateways flank a symbolic stairway to heaven, a long flight of ceremonial steps leading to three terraces. Rising from the top terrace was once a massive *lingam*, now in the Jakarta Museum, realistically carved as a phallus, which was the focus for rites celebrating the mysterious power of generation, human and cosmic.

Gargoyle spouts and drainage channels testify that the *lingam* would have been ritually lustrated with sacred liquids. One of the numerous, but tantalizing, inscriptions refers to 'the waters that deliver us into the boundless'.

Most striking are Sukuh's profuse carvings. They depict popular stories from the great Hindu epic *Mahabharata*; their prominent theme is liberation – from demons, curses, snakes, the bondage of the material world. Most significant is Bhima, a spiritual hero famed for his quest for esoteric knowledge and immortality, who overcomes the fires of hell and steals ambrosia from the gods. On one of the most interesting panels, he is portrayed as the archetypal blacksmith forging a *keris*, the magical dagger used as a supernatural talisman throughout the Indonesian archipelago. The smith's creative mastery of fire is a sacred skill; the phallic *keris* its supreme artefact. Indeed, as an embodiment of potent spiritual power, the snake-like *keris* is often combined with the *lingam*; such multiple associations make it a complex symbol of spiritual transformation, hinting at the exacting alchemy of purification undergone by practitioners of the *tantric* path of *kundalini* yoga.

Though their subjects are Hindu, the style of these carvings is unmistakably Javanese, employing the characteristic attenuation that derives from the spectral world of the *wayang*, Java's shadow puppet

'Every man in Java, rich or poor, must have a keris *in his house, and a lance and a shield, and no man between the ages of twelve and eighty may go out of doors without a* keris *in his belt.'*

TOME PIRES, EUROPEAN TRAVELLER, 1515

OPPOSITE AND THIS PAGE Stone reliefs at Mount Lawa: penis and vagina, hermaphroditic figure, a boar, and a *kirtimukha* 'face of glory'.

Sacred Sexuality

theatre. Angular, two-dimensional figures glide through a netherworld populated by strange and sometimes demonic apparitions, fugitive disembodied spirits, such as are invoked here.

But Sukuh's rituals were not only for the benefit of the departed. Contact with death throws one back into life with renewed vigour. Accordingly, much of the carving is erotic; particularly striking are the realistic phallus and vulva placed within a circle on the gateway. In tantric teachings, sexual rituals are used to galvanize the subtle energies of the body and transmute them into a state of consciousness beyond change and death. Such disciplines were always protected from the general public and limited to aspirants who fulfilled rigorous criteria of initiation.

Sukuh's sister site, Chandi Ceto, tells much the same story. Built in 1470, its original fourteen terraces were very delapidated when it was first excavated in 1928. The site has now been restored, with a Balinese-style gate on each terrace, images placed in small wooden shrines and a simple Hindu-Javanese-style altar. Happily, this modern neatness is undercut by the partly ruined eighth terrace. Here we find archaic representations of Bhima surrounded by a retinue of fantastic creatures representing the zodiac. Especially interesting are the magic cosmograms – three circles, two carved with nine-pointed stars and one with a seven-pointed star. Nearby is a tortoise, Chinese-derived symbol of the *axis mundi*, and a triangle set with a *lingam*. Such recondite symbols were used to link the priestly acolyte with distant realms. An embodiment of beauty, numinosity and sacerdotal knowledge, Chandi Ceto stands as the last great monument of south Asian spirituality erected in Java before the tidal wave of Islam all but submerged the Indian religions there.

ABOVE AND OPPOSITE
Steps descend from the pyramid of Chandi Ceto toward the split gates beyond Mount Lawa; at Chandi Sukuh architecture and water combine to create an atmosphere of great holiness.

Bali, Indonesia
An Island of Balance

THE ISLAND OF BALI, a lushly fecund outcrop in the Indonesian archipelago, is a uniquely coherent example of a sacred society. Measuring a mere 87 miles long by 56 wide, it is governed by its religion, Agama Hindu Bali, a mixture of ancient animistic beliefs and a pure form of early Hinduism. This teaches the Balinese that they are born into a matrix of various obligations – to the forces of nature, gods, ancestral souls, demons and fellow human beings – and that a good life comes from the recognition and fulfilment of these obligations. Co-operation in groups earns the support of almighty Nature, and the average Balinese will belong to family and territorial groups, as well as various functional organizations and voluntary associations, which will all call on his participation. In Bali, to be is to be related.

The foundation of this world-view is the delicate and always temporary balance between two essential and complementary forces: the heavenly (*kaja*) and the earthly (*kelod*). The supreme focus of heavenly power is Gunung Agung, the semi-active volcano that lies at the eastern end of the island. All the influences that flow from the great mountain downwards towards the sea, following the path of the rising sun from the east, are positive, fertile and divine. As the sun passes its zenith and sinks into the west, the earthly forces take over. These, seen as unpredictable, potentially dangerous and allied to change and death, flow in the opposite direction, from the sea upwards towards the mountain. Thus, throughout the island – home, field, temple – the highest and easternmost point is always the purest and most auspicious, the lowest and seaward the least pure and most dangerous.

As all aspects of life are governed by this dualistic scheme, everything is carefully oriented. In the family compound, the temple is in the *kaja* area, the rubbish tip in the *kelod*; one should always sleep with the head towards the east, but burial and cremation grounds and temples to the earth deities should be located downwards towards the sea. From the slopes of Gunung Agung flow waters to irrigate the rice, itself a sacramental substance as the staple food and the embodiment of Dewi Shri, goddess of fertility. People labour cooperatively; plant growth is encouraged by specific rites while negative influences and pests are banished from the fields by exorcism. Each field has its

'For me, art is those things that reveal a relationship between man and God.
Seen from another perspective, art is the mirror of religious thought.'

I GUSTI PUTU RAKA, BALINESE ARTIST

OPPOSITE AND THIS PAGE
Scenes from the shrines
of Puni Besakih in the
shadow of Gunung
Agung: a cloth wraps a
sacred stone; and a
full-moon ceremony
begins on the beach at
Ketewel.

An Island of Balance

bamboo shrine to the agricultural deities.

In order to keep the invisible forces in balance a complex body of religious ritual has been developed, the enactment of which takes the form of an oft-repeated drama. In this, the place of the rite becomes the stage, while the priests and helpers function as directors and stage hands and the believers are the actors playing their roles. The gods, for whose interest and pleasure the whole thing is being performed, form an invisible and highly critical audience, looking for a perfect presentation of the rite before they vouchsafe their considerable blessings. Dance, drama and music are almost as indispensable a part of this sacrificial ritual as the offering itself.

The Balinese are unceasing in their ritual attention to the souls of the dead, but anyone expecting to find gloomy mourning will be sorely disappointed. Funerals here are noisy and colourful celebrations of the fact that another *kaja* soul has finally been freed from the decaying prison of its *kelod* body. But ritual cremations are costly affairs. They involve a spectacular processional tower – made of wood, bamboo, coloured paper and cloth, tinsel, mirrors, and blossoms – not to mention the coffin (often in the shape of Shiva's bull), offerings, holy water and numerous guests to be entertained. So the body is often buried until there is enough money for the funeral. Several families may band together to finance a funeral; sometimes there is the possibility of joining the cremation of a rich or noble person, whose soul may generously take a hundred or more with it. In death, as in life, the parts must work together for the good of what is truly a commonwealth.

THIS PAGE AND OPPOSITE
The lower courtyard
from the Kori Agung
gate, Pura Pasar Agung;
merus near Rendang,
east Bali; temple
procession on Ketewel
Beach, with two young
girls in trance.

Shatrunjaya, North India
The Peaceful Liberators

THE FOUR MEN STROLLING nonchalantly through the dazzling white courtyard are naked except for white masks over their mouths and white fly-whisks in their hand, but they draw hardly a glance from the people around. Everything here is so essential and pristine – the walls exquisitely carved with figures, animals and geometric mandalas, the pavilions and balconies crowned with rusticated conical towers – that nakedness is in no way out of place; indeed, it seems somehow the appropriate way to participate. In fact, it emulates the radical simplicity of the spirit that these men, members of the Digamabara ('Sky Clad'), the most austere school of Jain monks, go naked, and have done so since long before Alexander the Great debated with them – he called them 'the gymnosophists'- during his aborted invasion of India in the 3rd century B.C. Their less ascetic brethren, the Shvetambara ('White Clad') are permitted simple white cotton robes, but they also must wear the cotton gauze masks that stop them inadvertently breathing in insects, and carry the soft cotton brushes to sweep tiny creatures out of their path as they walk. And walk they do; all Jain monks are forbidden by their vows from staying long in one place, and spend their lives on the move. For them the pilgrimages enjoined on all Jains are epecially important, adding structure and focus to their austere itinerant life.

Among the most ancient of religions, Jainism stretches back to at least 1000 B.C., through a tradition of twenty-four enlightened Masters called *jinas* ('conquerors') or *tirthankaras* ('those who have crossed to the other side'). The last of these, Mahavira, was probably contemporary with the Buddha, and the two faiths share much. Jainism was to influence all later Indian thought with its radical doctrines of non-violence and vegetarianism; Mahatma Gandhi took many of his ideas from it. Even farming is forbidden the faithful, lest they unwittingly kill small creatures, so lay Jains have always specialized in business, especially banking and the gem trade. Their resulting wealth, combined with an habitual piety, has made them the builders of some of the most beautiful temples on earth.

Those which all Jains most wish to visit before they die are the ones on the holy mountain of Shatrunjaya, 'The Place of Victory', that overlooks the scorching plains of Gujarat, cotton bowl of western India. Clustered along its twin summits stands a staggering collection of no less than 800 temples and shrines containing between them almost 5000 images. Shatrunjaya is a veritable citadel of the sacred, rising aloof above the ant-like scurry of the world below, its sacred structures grouped together in walled enclosures (*tuks*) that exude an almost military feel, giving no hint of the ornate splendours within.

> '*Spirit and non-spirit together constitute the universe.*
> *All that is necessary is to discriminate between them.*'
>
> MEDIEVAL JAIN TEXT

OPPOSITE AND THIS PAGE
Scenes from the Adinath temple: a silver chariot of a Jain teacher and elephant; offerings to images of *tirthankaras*; a garlanded *tirthankara*; a masked worshipper.

The Peaceful Liberators

The main and largest temple here is dedicated to Adinath, first of the *tirthankaras*. To enter the temple is like stepping into the organic perfection of matter itself; we are inside a faceted jewel, a snowflake or a cavern of salt-bleached coral. It is said that the masons were paid by the weight of the dust they chiselled out. Birds chirp and flutter happily among the fretted recesses, and the soft warm air is filled with the muted yet sonorous drone of prayers and chants, like the contented hum of pollen-heavy bees.

In the darkened holy of holies sits the image of Adinath, silvered eyes gleaming fitfully in the half light. An austere white marble figure seated in meditation, he could at first sight be mistaken for the Buddha, but the Buddha is never naked or shown with hair falling to his shoulders. Nor is this a 'deity' who will answer prayers or grant salvation; the image of a *tirthankara* serves rather as a meditational support, an ideal and exemplary model of the soul that embodies a state of liberation attainable, eventually, by all of us. In keeping with the pervasive air of simplicity there are no official priests here. An old woman, bent almost double, painstakingly performs her own ritual offerings. After prostrating, she carefully lights a stick of swirling incense, then pours a silver bowl of holy water over the adamantine figure, gently dabs fragrant sandalwood paste on various parts of his body, and finally scatters a handful of rose petals over his head, like blood-red tears brilliant in a shaft of sunlight.

Shatrunjaya, as so much of northern India, suffered devastation from the Muslim invasions of the 14th and 15th centuries, and all its structures here postdate that holocaust. But the rebuilt shrines show an unbroken stylistic continuity with earlier monuments, particularly those of the Solanki dynasty [11th–12th centuries A.D.], and we know that one ruler, Siddharaja Solanki [1095–1142] made particularly generous donations here in what was a golden age of temple building. Jain builders were generally happy to borrow auspicious deities from Hinduism, and Laxmi the Giver of Wealth, Saraswati the Goddess of Wisdom, the perennially popular Remover of Obstacles and the portly and mischievous Ganesh, are widely represented here, perhaps as a consolation for those of us not yet able to embark on the austere path of perfection laid down by the *tirthankaras*.

ABOVE AND OPPOSITE
Doli-wallahs carrying pilgrims leave the main gate of the Vimalavasi temple; the Vallabahi temple and the southern ridge.

Amritsar, North India
The Golden Temple of the Sikhs

Lying only fifteen miles from India's border with Pakistan, Amritsar is a wild frontier town. An ancient junction of the trade routes that wind their way laboriously across the roof of the world, it is a tribal rug of a place, its roughly variegated texture woven from all the nomadic strands of Central Asia – Turkomans, Iranians and Himalayan hill people mix with long-faced Kashmiris, Tibetans and Indians up from the plains. The mud streets of the bazaar resound with the clamour of the fierce tribesmen who have ruled the mountainous borders of Afghanistan and Pakistan for so long; their faces are those of warriors: bearded, swarthy and aloof. Their pointed sandals kick up the dust with embroidered leather as dry and as cracked as the mountain passes they have crossed to get here. Yet the bustle is not chaotic; the town exudes an atmosphere of energetic industry, and its population of one million seems well organized and prosperous. And this is just as it should be, for Amritsar is the sacred capital of one of India's most vigorous and united communities: the Sikhs.

Founded by Guru Nanak in 1497, Sikhism was an attempt to reconcile the teachings of Islam and the Hinduism it so persecuted in the sub-continent. A god-intoxicated poet and singer, Nanak was a religious revolutionary, travelling the country teaching against idolatory, superstition and priestly exploitation. He denounced all forms of inequality, including the caste system, and proclaimed the brotherhood of all humanity, irrespective of race, class or creed. Greatly influenced by the medieval mystic Kabir, a weaver from Varanasi who was one of India's most loved and influential saints, Nanak continued his tolerant teachings that God is one, beyond all form and divisions, accessible to all. He called the followers of his egalitarian creed Sikhs, from the Sanskrit *shishya,* meaning 'disciple', and on his death in 1539, Nanak founded the line of ten *gurus* that were to lead the emerging Sikh nation; he called them *khalsa* or 'Pure Ones'.

The heart of Amritsar is the Golden Temple, the Mecca of India's five million Sikhs. It dates from the time of the fifth *guru*, Ram Das [A.D. 1574–81] who established a shrine, still there today, on the site of an ancient healing spring known as the 'Pool of the Nectar of Immortality' and invited Sikh merchants to live around it. His son and successor, Guru Arjun, completed the temple in 1601; in keeping with the tolerant

'The waters first retained the golden embryo in which
all the gods were aggregated, single, deposited on the navel
of the unborn creator, in which all beings abide.'

RIG VEDA

OPPOSITE AND THIS PAGE
The Golden Temple, set in the Lake of Ambrosia; the processions of the Guru Granth Sahib scripture from the temple to the Akhal Takhat pavilion where it spends the night.

The Golden Temple of the Sikhs

attitude of the new faith, the foundation stone was laid by a local Muslim saint.

The Sikhs were persecuted almost continuously by the Mughals who ruled north India from 1526 until the coming of the British. Indeed Sikh history is one of struggle and martyrdom in defence of the temple. The greatest scourge of Amritsar itself was the Afghan freebooter Ahmad Shah Durani, who sacked the temple in 1751 and again in 1757. Ranjit Singh, 'Lion of the Punjab', the general who fought so fiercely against the British in the Sikh Wars, finalized the rebuilding and gave the temple its present form. In 1830 he donated 100 kgs of gold that was applied as gold leaf on copper plates covering the roof and both the outside and inside walls, surmounting dados of purest white marble.

It was the tenth *guru*, Gobindh Singh, who turned the *khalsa* into a fighting force. He died in 1708, decreeing that he would be the last in the line. Henceforward the spiritual focus of the faith would be the Guru Granth Sahib, the collection of hymns and songs composed by Kabir and the ten *gurus*. This book is the focus of the temple. It sits on a sumptuous flower-covered platform under a canopy studded with jewels; professional singers take turns singing verses from the book accompanied by musicians. This singing is continuous from 4 a.m. to 11 p.m. in summer; 5 a.m. to 10 p.m. in the cold Punjab winter. Each evening it is taken in a golden palanquin with an extravagant procession – golden canopy set with rubies, emeralds and diamonds, silver poles, strings of pearls, music – to spend the night in a domed temple in the complex. Throughout the day the tide of the faithful ebbs and flows past walls

decorated with plaster and set with mirrorwork, gold leaf, designs of birds and animals and flowers in twinkling semi-precious stones. The hypnotic richness of the chanting, the scent of incense and flowers and the human tapestry combine in an atmosphere of intense devotion.

The siting of the temple within its sacred tank serves several symbolic purposes. It stands for the island, a haven of calm in the midst of the ever-changing flux of life. With its four doors always kept open to the four directions, it is the central point of the Sikh universe. From here the transcendent sounds of the Guru Granth Sahib 'create' the world of time and space, dividing the cosmos into four, a division that orders the manifesting universe as it emerges from the womb of the absolute, the cosmic waters.

When it was built, the temple was likened by Guru Arjun to a ship that ferries people across the ocean of ignorance and suffering to the further shore of Enlightenment. As such it is the physical analogue of Pak Nam – the Name of God – on which Sikhs meditate, the mantra which takes the attention from the restless surface of the mind to the eternal calm of its innermost depths. Furthermore, covered in gold, the temple acts out the Vedic creation myth of the universe's emergence from the Golden Egg – Hiranyagarbha – that rests on the cosmic waters of infinite potential at the beginning of each successive cycle of creation. Thus, not only is a journey to the temple a voyage to the 'beginning of time', but, as always in sacred art, the pervasive use of gold represents the celestial light of the finest levels of creation, that level of life which is closest to the imageless purity of the Divine radiance itself.

ABOVE AND RIGHT Views at night and at sunrise towards the Golden Temple across its sacred tank, including one from the four-hundred-and-fifty-years-old Baba Gujhaji tree shrine.

THE PATH OF

THE SIXTH CENTURY B.C. was a time of profound significance for the East. The Vedic civilization in India was in a state of decline at just the time a new and powerful urban mercantile class was emerging. This new group felt alienated from the arcane and exclusive practices of Hindu orthodoxy, the closed world of the *brahmin* priests with their domination of religious life through recondite texts, sacrificial rites and the caste system. The time was ripe for change, and it came in the form of a teacher the world was to know as the Buddha.

The Buddha did not deny the existence of the gods of Vedic Hinduism, but taught that they were not germane to the prime endeavour of the religious life, which was the understanding and conquest of suffering. His approach was to reject all philosophical theory, all belief, and return people to the essential spiritual task of purifying one's own mind by transcending the self-centredness and cravings that poison behaviour. He called his message the *dharma*: 'that which upholds life'.

He also rejected the caste system and priestly Sanskrit, teaching in the

ENLIGHTENMENT
In the Footsteps of the Buddha

vernacular, and though he probably saw himself as a reformer, the Buddha was not concerned with founding a religion. He likened himself to a doctor who diagnoses the illness and prescribes the cure, and wished only to establish a monastic order (*sangha*) of men and women who would be able to take the medicine of his teachings and find out the truth for themselves.

Travelling, teaching and establishing communities all over north-east India until his death in 544 B.C. at the age of 80, he strongly discouraged any personal adulation; it was only after his death that his followers began to organize what we call the Buddhist religion. Patronized by the wealthy merchant classes, this spread rapidly, and with the conversion of the Mauryan Emperor, Ashoka, in the middle of the 3rd century B.C., its future as a major spiritual and cultural force was assured, reaching Sri Lanka (*c.* 240 B.C.), Burma (*c.* 235 B.C.), Vietnam (*c.* 40 B.C.), Thailand (*c.* A.D. 300), Indonesia (*c.* 4th century), Laos and Cambodia (*c.* 5th century).

Bodh Gaya, India
The Garden of Enlightenment

MORE THAN FIVE HUNDRED years before Christ, a solitary seeker after truth arrived here at Bodh Gaya. This wandering mendicant was the thirty-five-year-old Prince Gautama, who had renounced his throne seven years earlier to embark on a lonely journey that had taken him, fruitlessly, from teacher to teacher. Arriving here in the sacred grove, he took a seat under a venerable fig tree, and vowed not to leave until he had attained full Enlightenment.

As the May full moon rose brilliant in the sky, Gautama settled into deep meditation, as he had so many times before, transcending level after level of sensation, thought and feeling, to leave behind all that could be described as a limited personal self. He saw clearly not only the workings of his own mind, but the events of his previous births. As the final liberation of *nirvana* dawned, Gautama was challenged by Mara, the Tempter, epitome of the blinding force of ignorance. Refusing his offers of wordly enjoyments and riches, the young man was questioned as to the stability of his newly-realized state of freedom. Calling the Mother Earth to be his witness, he touched the ground in front of him with his right hand. At that spot the goddess arose, wrung out her long wet hair and the resulting flood swept Mara and his army away. Rainbows and lights appeared in the sky, and all the celestial beings rejoiced, showering down flowers upon the earth in celebration. From this point the prince was known as the Buddha, an impersonal title meaning 'He who has woken up'.

Bodh Gaya is the Buddhist paradise garden, but it is not like Eden, watched over by a stern father-god, nor does it have the intellectual order of the Islamic heaven. It is unmistakably Indian: a higgledy-piggledy place, an untamed jungle of creepers and bushes, gnarled stumps and twisted roots. The ground is littered with little clay votive lamps, burnt twists of wick, stubs of incense. Everywhere stand stone *stupas* and monuments erected by kings and commoners alike from all over the Buddhist world, mute witnesses to the universality of the Master's message. Each has its own place, size and height,

LEFT Festoons around the most sacred tree of Buddhism, the *bodhi* at Bodh Gaya under which the Master achieved *nirvana.*

ABOVE AND OPPOSITE
The Mahabodhi temple:
a gilded image of the
Buddha in
dharmachakra mudra,
the pose of his first
discourse; a Burmese
monk performs
circumambulation.

The Garden of Enlightenment

much like the different forms of Buddhism catering to the varying needs and abilities of humanity. Here, as so often in India, the juxtaposition of stone and vegetation brings surprise and delight. In and out of this leafy tangle float monks, striking as exotic butterflies – Tibetans in deep burgundy, Sri Lankans in saffron, Burmese in burnished amber, Japanese in jet black.

What first catches the visitor's attention is not the tree but the Mahabodhi ('Great Enlightenment') temple which was built next to it. The present structure dates from the second century A.D., erected on the site of one built almost five hundred years earlier by the great Emperor Ashoka, whose patronage turned the Buddha's teaching into a state religion. The Chinese monk and intrepid traveller, Hieuen-tsang, tells us in his diaries that the temple was 'carved with several niches, each of which contains a gilded statue of the Buddha. On all four sides the walls are covered with beautiful sculptures, festoons of pearls and figures of sages; the architraves and pillars, the doors and the windows are all ornamented with gold and silver casings, among which pearls and precious stones are inserted'. He also mentions two solid silver images, about ten feet high, which have long since gone. Repairs and enlargements over the centuries culminated in 1884 with the British finishing the most recent restoration, begun by the Burmese kings in 1811. Essentially a truncated pyramid surrounded by four miniature replicas of the central spire in each of the cardinal points, the temple radiates the influence of the teaching out to all corners of the universe, and is topped by a finial shaped like the segmented *amalaka* fruit, a symbol of *nirvana*.

And so to the tree – a type of inedible fig the Indians call *peepal*, and botanists classify as *ficus religiosa*. It is popularly known as the *bodhi* (or *bo*) tree, the 'Tree

of Enlightenment'. A descendant of the original, it really is extraordinarily protective. Here under its widespread branches, which seem to embrace all humanity, there is a constant and quiet devotion, very different to the noisy activity of many Hindu temples. In the shaded tranquillity the mind really does begin to settle down, becoming still enough to notice things normally overlooked, sights and sounds usually blotted out by the habitual chattering of thought that prevents us from living in the present moment.

It is fitting that the Buddha attained *nirvana* at the roots of a tree. His original teaching was a radical restatement of the ancient wisdom of life, undercutting the whole corrupted edifice of priests, rituals and gods. His message was to get to the roots of our own minds, for our life is but the extension of our thinking and feeling, and the goal of the real happiness we all seek lies deep within ourselves, not in endless manipulation, or even experience, of the outside world. The tool for this exploration is meditation, which establishes a basis of inner silence, from which the mind can see calmly and clearly, unclouded by fear, expectation or projection. Any other approach to the problems of life is ultimately only cosmetic – like the gardener who tries to nourish a wilting plant by polishing its leaves. The intelligent approach is to water the root, and the whole plant will naturally flourish. As awareness of reality grows, there is no abandoning of those who are suffering; on the contrary, insight must be accompanied by loving kindness, the mind balanced by the heart. It is fitting that the leaf of the *peepal* is heart-shaped, a gentle reminder of the importance of love and compassion, lest we abandon humanity in our search for divinity and eventual Enlightenment.

Anuradhapura, Sri Lanka
Planting the Seed of Truth

AROUND 500 B.C., Aryan invaders from north India arrived in the island known as Ratnadvipa, 'the Island of Jewels', to create a magnificent and scrupulously organized capital at the site now known as Anuradhapura. A Royal Palace stood surrounded by four suburbs to accommodate the four major castes, the city was filled with shrines and hospitals, and employed several hundred undertakers, street cleaners and sewerage workers. An extraordinarily sophisticated system of reservoirs, linked by over 600 miles of channels, fed the city and the adjacent 'dry zone' of the island. The *Mahavamsa*, Sri Lanka's 'Great Chronicle', adds that the people were highly religious, worshipping *yakshas* – deities of water, mountains and fertility – ancestors and tribal chiefs, and various sacred trees, among which were the *banyan*, tamarind and palmyra palm.

Then, in the third century B.C., the island was galvanized by the arrival of Buddhism. Ashoka the Great, ruler of an empire that stretched from Mysore to the Himalayas and from

*'As they treat the remains of kings,
so Ananda, should they treat the remains
of an Enlightened One.
At the four crossroads a cairn
should be erected to an Enlightened One.
And whosoever shall place
there garlands, perfumes, or paints,
or make salutations there,
or become in its presence calm in heart,
that shall long be to them a profit
and a joy.'* THE BUDDHA'S INSTRUCTION

TO HIS FAVOURITE DISCIPLE ANANDA.

LEFT A schoolgirl walks silhouetted against the sunrise over the Bassawakkuluma tank and the Ruvanelisaya *dagoba*.

Planting The Seed of Truth

ABOVE AND OPPOSITE
Prayer flags hang
from a *bodhi* tree in
Anuradhapura;
schoolgirls pass by
against the backdrop
of the Abhayagiri
dagoba.

Afghanistan to Bangladesh, had converted to Buddhism. Under his tireless patronage, Buddhism became both a state religion and a potent proselytizing force through all south-east Asia. It was Ashoka's son, the monk Mahinda, who brought the *dharma* to Sri Lanka. Arriving in 230 B.C., he converted King Tissa, who begged him to come to his capital Anuradhapura with his fellow monks. They are said to have levitated there, arriving 'by air' outside the east gate of the city. So brilliant was Mahinda that 500 women were converted from his first discourse in the Royal Palace; so great was the demand to hear the *dharma* that the royal elephant stables were then turned into an audience hall and a further thousand people converted. Moving outside the city to the Mahamega gardens, Mahinda continued his work; according to the *Mahavamsa* chronicle, 'the lightgiver' in this way brought 8,500 to the *dharma* in the space of only seven days. The gardens later became the site of Anuradhapura's principal monastery, the Mahavihara.

The king then sent a novice monk to bring the Buddha's right collar bone relic from India. The relic was housed in the first recorded *dagoba* (an abbreviation of *dhatu-garbha*: 'relic-womb', that is the Singhalese word for *stupa*). This was the Thuparama, built in the shape of a heap of paddy, a fertility symbol associated with peace and plenty. Other *stupas* followed rapidly, like mushrooms springing up after the long-awaited rains. The most magnificent was the great white-domed 'bubble shape', Ruwanweli Dagoba, set in the midst of the Mahavihara monastery complex; later came the 'lotus shape' and 'bell shape'. Each had, in varying proportions, four elements: base, dome, intermediate square member known as the *harmika* and finial. The height of the first three elements should be the same, each

three-fifths of the total diameter of the ground plan. The dome, in which the relics are kept, is known as the *anda* ('egg'), an image alluding to the quickening potential of the relic, and to the golden egg from which the universe emerged.

Mahinda's next move was to send for his sister, the nun Sanghamitta, who brought a cutting of the original *bodhi* tree from Bodh Gaya. The King himself watered it daily from vessels made of gold and silver, and it replaced all the other trees then in worship. More than twenty-two hundred years old, a descendant of this tree is still the most sacred spot in Sri Lanka, fulfilling the prophecy that it 'would flourish and be green for ever'. Hereditary decendants of the guardians first appointed by King Tissa still attend to it. Protected by golden railings, it has spawned many other *bodhi* trees from its roots, and most of the other *bodhi* trees on the island, as well as those in Burma and Thailand, have been grown from its seeds. A potent symbol of the enduring spread of the *dharma*, the tree continues to inspire: at Poson, the May full-moon festival, over a million worshippers come to celebrate the Enlightenment.

Today Anuradhapura is an atmospheric open-air museum. Palaces, monasteries, *stupas*, image-houses, monastic quarters, chapter-houses, tanks, baths and irrigation works all lie open to the sky. The city inspired many prototypical designs of *stupa* and image; perhaps its greatest achievement came in about 88 B.C., when the sacred texts of Theravada Buddhism were first written down, in the Pali language, as a defence against schisms in the order. This crucial moment ensured that the religion would never die, and its consequent spread as a major global force was due to the fact that here in the heart of the Island of Jewels its traditions, texts and faith were safely preserved.

Temple of the Tooth, Sri Lanka
Power of the Relic

GIVEN ITS SANCTITY, the Tooth of the Buddha has had a violent history. Originally smuggled from India in the tresses of a princess, the relic was taken as talisman to Sri Lanka's first Buddhist capital Anuradhapura. Then, after various kidnappings and transfers, including an attempted snatch by the Chinese and a spell back in India at the time Marco Polo arrived on the island, it was stolen in the sixteenth century by the Portuguese. In a fit of Catholic righteousness, they took it to their Indian colony of Goa and ceremoniously burned it, grinding the ashes to powder and casting them into the sea. But that relic, say the Sinhalese, was a copy. The genuine one was kept safe, and is now enshrined in the Dalada Maligava in Kandy, a splendid temple built by a succession of Kandyan kings from A.D. 1687 onwards.

Today the temple, an imposing columned building stuccoed in pink, roofed in gold leaf and surrounded by a moat, overlooks the tranquil Kandy Lake. It is the centrepiece of the Royal Palace area, a small complex of buildings which is all that remains of what was Sri Lanka's final bastion of Buddhist civilization.

The capital of Sri Lanka for over three hundred years since the fall of Polonnaruwa, Kandy resisted all the colonial advances of the Portuguese and then the Dutch, nations still remembered with hatred in local folk songs for the appalling damage they did. But in 1815 this proud resistance was finally broken when the British took the town. Considering another religion to be mere superstition, colonial officials imperiously opened up the golden relic caskets. They discovered the hallowed object was indeed a tooth, but almost two inches long. Whatever its true status, the Tooth is preserved, along with magnificent jewellery gifted by successive Kandyan kings, within a golden casket

*'And for seven days the lord of the land held this great feast in honour of
the three sacred objects – the Buddha, the* dharma *and the* sangha *–
in such a manner as if he were showing here on earth how even the chief of the gods
held the feasts of the Buddha in heaven...'*

THE MAHAVAMSA

OPPOSITE AND THIS PAGE
The casket of the sacred tooth relic, hung with jewels from the kings of Kandy; an elephant bas-relief at the shrine's entrance; drummers at the shrine just before it is opened to the public.

Power of the Relic

that is enclosed by a series of several golden *stupa*-shaped reliquaries, one within the other. Each casket is locked; the keys kept by the Diva Nilame, Keeper of the Shrine, and the senior monks of the island's two most important monasteries, the Asigirya and Malvatte.

While the Tooth itself is not exhibited to the public, daily worship is performed in its honour. The cleverly stage-managed drama of the *darshan* is intense. The sense of expectation – increased, rather than diminished, by the invisibility of its object – is heightened by the insistently hypnotic beating of drums and blowing of shawms,

ABOVE AND OPPOSITE
Musicians at the temple create the appropriate atmosphere for the worship of the tooth relic.

the flickering half-light of coconut-oil lamps and the fiercely protective glare of the attendant priests, tensed ready to discipline the undulating crowd if necessary.

But such strictly contained solemnity is only half the picture: the other is carnival. The relic (though some say only a replica) is brought out into the fresh air and processed around the city once a year at the Perahera festival, two weeks of truly spectacular celebration culminating on the full-moon of Shravana (July/August). The Perahera was originally a Hindu festival to honour the island's four protective deities: Shiva, Vishnu, Karttikeyya and the Virgin Goddess. When the Tooth arrived here it was happily incorporated into the festival procession, demonstrating the fact that Hinduism and Buddhism, from the indigenous point of view, are fundamentally two aspects of one faith.

Much of the extraordinary original splendour of the Perahera remains. Kandy has always been famous for its musicians, and thousands of drummers, dancers and performers lead the procession, cracking whips, waving banners, leaping wildly in the air. They are followed by other equally celebrated local inhabitants, the elephants. Magnificently caparisoned in cloths appliquéd with gold and silver thread, perhaps a hundred of these noble beasts amble past, their leader bearing the relic casket in a ceremonial and canopied howdah.

Next come members of Kandy's royal aristocracy, attired in white-cotton *lungi* sarongs or pantaloons, topped by velvet sequined jackets and ceremonial gold turbans, and hung with creamy garlands of jasmine and frangipani. Each dignitary, protected by a ceremonial parasol of crimson, white and gold, is accompanied by huge royal fans decorated in the design of the eight-petalled lotus of Buddhism.

Polonnaruwa, Sri Lanka
Medieval Capital of the Faith

FEW PEOPLE TODAY have heard of George Turnour, but it is due to the dedicated labours of this little-known scholar that we know so much of the refined Buddhist civilization of Sri Lanka. One of those gifted and passionate amateurs who fell in love with their host culture, Turnour was a government agent for the British Raj in Ratnapura who became fascinated by the island's history, especially what he heard of the *Mahavamsa*, an mysterious chronicle whose existence was known only to a handful of Buddhist monks. A hundred books of palm-leaf manuscript, the *Mahavamsa* covered an astonishing twenty-three centuries, from 543 B.C. to A.D. 1758, spread over the reigns of 163 sovereigns. Written in codified metrical Pali verses, it remained untranslated, and it was only after a painstaking search of all Sri Lanka's temples and monasteries that Turnour eventually uncovered the *tike*, a code to unlock the ancient record.

The *Mahavamsa* confirmed what Turnour and others had long suspected, that after the mighty Anuradhapura had declined, the island's capital moved to Polonnaruwa, a lost city long hidden in the deep jungles that cover the north-east of the island. Rediscovered by a British army officer in 1820, Polonnaruwa was shown to have been a royal residence since the seventh century and the seat of the Chola invaders from Tamil Nadu in south India in the eleventh century. Then, in the latter half of the twelfth century, new life was breathed into the place by the greatest of all Sri Lankan monarchs, Parakramabahu I, after his brilliant military campaigns liberated the island from the Tamils.

The new king first set about nationalizing the lucrative export trade in gems and spices on which the island's stability depended. He developed the 'Sea of Parakrama', an extensive

'Not even a little of the water that comes from the rain must flow into the ocean without being made useful to man.'

PARAKRAMABAHU IN THE MAHAVAMSA CHRONICLE

LEFT Monumental granite statues of the Buddha at Gal Vihara, Polonnaruwa; on the left he stands after the Enlightenment; on the right he lies on the verge of death.

Medieval Capital of the Faith

irrigation system of interlinked tanks, the largest of which was nine miles square, that fed an area of thirty square miles of intensive paddy cultivation around the capital. The south-west coastal region was drained and planted with coconut palms which, then as now, supplied a host of everyday necessities: nutritious food and drink, timber, thatching, matting, rope and sacking, as well as many household utensils, charcoal, soap, fuel and oil for lamps and cooking.

Archaeological clearing begun in 1900 revealed Polonnaruwa to be another of his practical achievements. It was an enormous city, heavily influenced by Tamil building styles of brick and stucco and circumscribed by a four-mile outer wall inside which parks, hospitals, almshouses, Hindu temples, Buddhist image houses and *dagobas*, shops, tanks and extensive residences were grouped. At its heart lay the area known as the Great Quadrangle, where many of the city's loveliest buildings can still be seen, poignantly enhanced by their present semi-ruined state. The island's architecture gained a new dimension here, the use of lime mortar and joisted barrel vaulting enabling new heights of construction.

The Watadage or 'Round Shrine of the Relics' shows a pattern that was common. The main building was protected by carved creatures common in Buddhist symbolism – elephants, lions, wild geese, serpent door-guardians – and covered by an overarching conical roof of wood and tiles supported by stone pillars, the only part of the superstructure remaining. The shrine here has gracefully carved stairways, its inner part enclosing a low domed *dagoba* with Buddha figures facing outwards to the four directions. The proportion and judicious contrast between decorated and unworked surfaces are masterly. In the Nissanka Lata Mandapa,

'King Nissanka's Flower Altar', the eight pillars surrounding the miniature *dagoba* are undulating *art nouveau* lotus stems made of granite; their inscriptions tell us that Parakrama's successor, Nissanka, came here to listen to the monks chant the sacred Pali texts.

At the Gal Vihara, 'Rock Shrine', lying north of the Great Quadrangle, is a group of four massive sculptures in beautifully striated granite, whose self-confident treatment is tempered by a monumental sensitivity. Originally housed in wooden shrines long since gone, each displays the sensitive yet sober grandeur that is the hallmark of the Polonnaruwa style. The first two are the Buddha in *dhyana mudra*, the posture of meditation. One is seated on a throne decorated with lions and thunderbolts and surrounded by a halo. The other is flanked by the Hindu deities Brahma and Vishnu and surmounted by the sacred parasol denoting both temporal and spiritual authority.

Next, over seven metres tall, comes an unusual representation of the Master, standing with arms folded across his heart. It refers to the textual account of how the Buddha, transfixed by bliss and compassion for the suffering of humanity, spent the second week of the Enlightenment standing by the *bodhi* tree, 'without blinking'. The last piece, fully fourteen metres long, represents the *parinibbana*, or death of the Master. Lying on its right side, the figure is covered by a liquidly flowing robe and exudes an aura of extraordinary serenity. A fitting tribute to the royal patron is an inscription here that tells us how, at the time the Muslims were ruthlesly driving Buddhism out of its homeland, Parakrama successfully struggled to unite the Sinhalese monks into one 'Supreme Order', to keep the light of the *dharma* and the Buddhist faith alive in his island kingdom.

Pagan, Burma
Field of the Cloth of Saffron

O N THE EAST BANK of the mighty Irrawaddy river in central Burma stands Pagan. At its height [A.D. 1050 – 1290] Pagan boasted a staggering 13,000 religious buildings spread over an area of 40 square kilometres; today well over 2,000 remain, stretching majestically as far as the eye can see across the flat alluvial plain. Especially when lit by the rising or setting sun, the vista is breathtaking.

The rise of Pagan was the culmination of a long period of ethnic and religious intermixture. The indigenous Mon people of lower Burma were followers of Theravada Buddhism while upper Burma patronized the Mahayana, in particular a decadent sect of wild Tibetan *tantrikas* known as the Ari, who wore their hair long, rode horseback into battle and drank hard liquor. Their spiritual outlook had much of the magical animism favoured by the Burmese cult of *nat* spirits. Into this heady cultural mix stepped a young pretender called Anawrahta. His father had been forced to retire to a monastery after a failed coup; he himself was destined to die on the horns of a wild water-buffalo, but in his short life he was to build the foundations of a mighty empire. In 1044 he defeated the ruler of upper Burma in single combat and ascended the throne of Pagan. According to the *Glass Palace Chronicle*, the principal Burmese history, Anawrahta requested the king of Thaton, the capital of southern Burma, for one of his thirty sets of the *Tripitaka*, the complete Pali scriptures. Furious when his request was refused, Anawrahta assembled an army. The southern king, his ministers and all the skilled experts from his court were captured and the royal stable of thirty-two sacred white elephants loaded up with holy relics and scriptures.

With the royal order of Theravadin monks in tow, Anawrahta, now ruler of the whole country, returned in triumph to his capital. The captured scholars, priests and artisans, plus a labour force of some thirty thousand, were put to work to create Pagan. Its flowering created the greatest period in Burmese art. Two main categories of building predominate here: *stupas*, (known as *pagodas* or *zedis* in Burma) so numerous and varied they constitute a textbook of styles, and temples to house images of the Buddha and accommodate worshippers.

The builders of Pagan enthusiastically employed the radiating or 'true' arch in preference to the corbelling techniques found all over India; as a result monumentally stable buildings were constructed. Brick was the chief material

LEFT 'The Reclining Buddha', signifying the Master at the point of death; this statue was ordered by the captive King Manuha in 1057.

Field of the Cloth of Saffron

used, and though mud rather than lime mortar was favoured, the jointing was fine enough to allow for solid masses of load-bearing masonry 200 feet or more in height. Stone was used for trim, and the whole exterior protected from the weather by stucco coating which, to judge from what survives, was exquisitely decorative.

Greatest of all of Anawrahta's buildings was the mighty Shwezigon Pagoda, built to house a sacred tooth relic recently acquired from Tathon. The *Glass Palace Chronicle* tells us that the relic was placed in a jewelled casket on the back of a sacred white elephant; the animal was then let loose, where it stopped being deemed as the auspicious place to build the monument. The Shwezigon served as a model for innumerable *pagodas* throughout the country. The huge base is comprised of a pyramidal mass of terraces

ABOVE, RIGHT AND OVERLEAF Spires and model *bodhi* trees soar upwards at the Schwezigon Pagoda; a brick *pagoda* at Ywahassnggyi, Pagan; sunrise over south Gu Ni from north Gu Ni.

– the lower square, the upper circular – set with gateways, stairways and miniature spires and carrying a series of enamelled earthenware plaques with scenes from the *jatakas* – stories of the Buddha's previous lives. The whole structure is topped off with a relatively small bell-shaped *stupa* crowned by a jewel-studded *hti* parasol. The most impressive bronzes at Pagan, four twelve-foot Buddhas representing Shakyamuni and three of his predecessors, stand in the four shrines facing the stairways at the cardinal points.

The Ananda Temple, built around 1091 by Kyanzittha, the greatest of Anawrahta's successors, is one of the few temples here to have been under continuous worship for almost a thousand years. Again, four large gateways at the cardinal points open into a spacious walled courtyard in which the temple stands. Essentially, this is a massive cube with a long gabled portico on each side, forming a symmetrical Greek cross with arms nearly 300 feet long. Inserted in its massive walled outer corridor is a series of stone reliefs of the principal events in the Buddha's life. Glowing gilt and cinnabar in the subdued light, their simple and animated grace places them among the greatest of Burmese sculptures. Above the central cube, terraces lead to a tall gilded spire in the typical Burmese style: a slightly bulging *shikhara* derived from the temples of India, topped with an elongated bell-shaped dome leading to a finial with a golden *hti*, 170 feet above the ground.

A delicate balance of intricate detail and authoritative mass, the Ananda soars skyward. The inmost shrine in each of its four sides contains a colossal gilded Buddha, towering above the kneeling worshippers. Tiny hidden windows high up in the walls bathe each image in a subtle golden light, while its enigmatic smile radiates compassion.

ABOVE AND RIGHT
Cramped quarters for
a Buddha symbolize
King Manuha's
imprisonment;
a standing gilded
Buddha, original of
four images at the
Ananda Temple; prayers
before Buddha at the
Htilominlo Temple.

Shwedagon Pagoda, Burma
Memorial of Gold

IT WAS A SIMPLE gift, but welcome: little cakes made of honey. The young man seated beneath the ancient tree accepted it with a gentle smile, and the two brothers who offered it felt this silent exchange was the portent of something momentous. By way of thanks, the young man plucked eight hairs from his head and offered them in return. Thus did the newly-enlightened Buddha receive the first gift from his disciples and reward them with a sacred memento.

The two brothers, merchants from Okkala in Burma, began the return to their homeland, bearing the precious hairs to their king, Okkalapa. It was his dream many months previously, that a new Buddha was about to reach *nirvana*, which had sent them on their mission to India. They were to suffer many hardships on the voyage back. Two of the hairs were stolen by an envious king, two more taken by the King of the Serpents, who rose from his sea-bed kingdom to capsize their boat.

Arriving back, they were met with a great celebration attended by all the gods and *nats*. When the king opened the relic box, all eight hairs were miraculously found in place. As the king gazed at them, the hairs emitted a radiant light, seen for miles, that caused the deaf to hear and the blind to see. Rainbows appeared in the sky, flowers and gemstones rained down on the earth. In great joy, the pious king ordered that nested *pagodas* of iron, marble, lead, copper, tin and silver be built over the casket, and the whole lot covered by a *pagoda* of solid gold. Thus was born the mighty Shwedagon, the holiest *pagoda* in Burma.

The gold is everywhere. It begins as you climb the long covered stairway leading to the *pagoda*, a dark tunnel lined with wayside booths overflowing with pilgrim goods and votive offerings. Melodious gongs and the harsh rustle of new silks fill air already heavy with the scent of flowers and incense. Golden lights wink and glint in the darkness – flickering candles, smouldering joss-sticks and glowing cheroots reflect off the mirrors and sequins that bejewel teak carvings and appliquéd hangings. Golden Buddha images sit on golden thrones, cooled by golden fans, protected by golden parasols. The pilgrims add more gold in the shape of little squares of gold-leaf which, detached by asthmatic fans labouring to cool the sultry air, are wafted here and there, scintillating like fireflies, to alight with thistledown caresses on one's skin and clothing. And when, finally, the long dark shaft leads on to the blinding expanse of terrace, there is the Shwedagon itself, a volcano of gold rising over 300 feet against the blue sky.

The intial impression is overwhelming. The massive main structure, set on a succession of terraces, is surrounded by over a hundred others – pavilions, resting places, temples, shrines, guardian figures, oracle posts, commemorative *pagodas* of every shape and size – each with its own history, myths and rituals. So wide is the terraced platform on which all this sits that there is no sense of crowding. The sky overhead is vast, even though punctured with elegant needles of white and gold spires sweeping upwards alongside traditionally stepped wooden roofs of five, seven or nine fretted tiers. Everywhere there is activity, as groups and individuals glide purposefully from shrine to shrine: some

OPPOSITE AND THIS PAGE
Boys, dressed as the young Gautama arrive for the *shin-pyu* ceremony, prior to becoming novices; a devotee at the Wish-Fulfilling Place telling *mala* beads; sunrise over the *pagodas* of the Shwedagon.

Memorial of Gold

bowing, some kneeling, some bending, all with an unthinking natural grace and each and every one sartorially impeccable as only the Burmese know how. Dapper turbans, sarongs, blouses, waistcoats sway past, though the visitor may be surprised by the vivid yellow turmeric powder caked on the womens' faces as protection from the sun, or the sight of a monk smoking what Kipling called 'a whackin' great cheroot'.

Such is the profusion of buildings jostling for attention that the unschooled visitor would assume there is no overall plan. But plan in the Orient is organic not imposed, emerging in its own time out of the overall flow of life. Plan there certainly is, though, as so often in the East, and it is best appreciated from an aerial perspective. The basic module is the holy number eight and its multiples, corresponding to the Eightfold Noble Path

ABOVE AND OPPOSITE Views of the central *pagoda* at the Shwedagon: from the Wish-Fulfilling Place at sunset; from the octagonal terrace, restricted to male worshippers.

that is the core of the Master's teaching, and the eight-fold division of the universe – four cardinal points and four mid-points – through which the *dharma* is disseminated to all infinity. The epicentre of this mandala is the Shwedagon, or more properly, the relics it houses. The huge octagonal base of the *pagoda*, nearly 1,500 feet in circumference, has opposite each of its facets eight smaller *pagodas*. Of these sixty-four, the four largest front the four approach stairways that are aligned to the cardinal points. At each of the platform's four corners are fantastic guardians: sphinx-like creatures (*manokthihas*) and leo-gryphs (*chinthes*). Eight planetary posts form another surrounding circle, each corresponding to one of the eight days of the Burmese week and the eight associated auspicious animals. The pilgrim will immediately go to which post governs his birth and horoscope and make offerings, lustrate the adjacent Buddha figure and add flowers, fruit, and incense to the heaps already there. Next comes a visit to the shrines of the thirty-seven *nats*, indigenous spirits here long before Buddhism arrived and always demanding to be placated. Especially important is the shrine of Bo Bo Gyi, the *nat* Guardian of the Shwedagon. Then come the numerous pavilions, patronized by various communities and filled with marble Buddha images.

It is only much later that one can absorb the statistics so loved by the guide-books. The main *pagoda* is plated with 8,688 slabs of solid gold, and the tip of its spire, set with 5,448 diamonds and 2,317 precious stones – rubies, sapphires and topaz – is set with a huge emerald to catch the first and last rays of the sun. The parasol finial tinkles with tiny bells – 1,065 of gold and 420 of silver. All in all, the Shwedagon is truly a wonder.

LEFT AND ABOVE
The great variety of
Buddha statues in this
huge complex: an
image must always
be placed higher than
the worshippers; the
'headband' is a
distinctive feature of
the Burmese style.

Sagaing, Burma
The Power of Community

HALF AN HOUR'S RIDE in a ramshackle bus, south-west of Mandalay, lies Sagaing, the living centre of Buddhism in Burma today. The town was the capital of an independent state governed by Shan tribes from the fall of Pagan in 1315 until the centre of power moved to Innwa in 1364, and then briefly from 1760 to 1764 it was again the most important city of the kingdom.

Today, the group of hills rising gently up from the west bank of what Kipling famously called 'the Road to Mandalay', the arterial Irrawaddy river, has an atmosphere far removed from involvement with the centres of worldly power. They have become instead a veritable citadel of the sacred, dotted with some 600 monasteries, an important monastic hospital, and many shrines, temples and *pagodas*. Many are of a considerable age: Padamya Zedi dates from 1300, the impressive Soon U Ponya Shin Paya, from which a superb view of Sagaing can be had, from 1312. Such longevity stems from the fact that permanent materials such as masonry and brick were reserved almost exclusively for sacred buildings; secular buildings, and even palaces, were built of wood, often being dismantled and moved around the country when the court changed location.

The area around Sagaing was once notorious for the Naga tribal headhunters, today the only heads it produces are those of Buddha images, for the place is Burma's main source of marble, and the community's workshops are full of its cool whiteness, boldly offset by brilliant colours and gilding. The commonest form of the Buddha here is the 'Earth-touching' posture, the *bhumisparsha mudra*, which recalls the newly enlightened sage's defeat of Mara, the Tempter, and his spirit army. This posture is particularly popular throughout south-east Asia, perhaps because the story could well be used to illustrate how the incoming faith was superseding local animistic cults.

Over five thousand monks and nuns live in these frangipani-scented hills. Stairways and shadowed colonnades mark out the paths of the faithful, along which the flash of orange or delicate pink robes alternates with the white and purple of bougainvillea and the dark green leaves of the mango tree. At each time of the day the panorama undergoes subtle changes. In the misty early morning the hillside is threaded with saffron lines of barefoot monks (*pongyis*) out on their dawn alms-round. During this they collect all the food for their one daily meal, eaten before noon, and must accept anything that is put in the bowl. This custom has persisted unbroken for over twenty-five hundred years, since the days of the early community of disciples. It enacts an ancient arrangement of reciprocal benefit – little understood in the secular world where contemplation is not valued – whereby monks provide spiritual nourishment to society and the lay population in turn provides material support to the contemplative order. The householder works on the gross, active level of life, dealing with the happiness and sorrow of job and family. His donations – daily food, items of practical use in the monastery, gifts at birthdays and festivals, images to the temple – ensure that his good *karma* is increased. The monk, on the other hand, works on the subtle, hidden level of life through meditative discipline and practice, thereby purifying and

OPPOSITE AND THIS PAGE The life of young nuns at the Zay Yar Theingi Gyaung convent: the study of scriptures; preparing meals for the annual *kathin* robes presentation; at daily study.

ABOVE AND RIGHT
Monks at Hintha Giri
monastery wait
patiently for a donation
of food at a rice
presentation ceremony;
pagodas on the main
ridge line of the
Sagaing hills at dusk.

The Power of Community

enhancing not only his, but also the
collective consciousness.

At midday, Sagaing's gilded spires (*htis*)
are brilliantly picked out by the high sun –
perhaps it was vistas such as this that gave
Burma its ancient name of Suvarnabhumi
– 'Land of Gold' – and the heavy warm air
is filled with the chanting of scriptures
and prayers drifting up from the
monasteries. And as the day cools and the
light fades rapidly in the short tropical
dusk, the restful hill twinkles with the
lights of buildings and fires, and the air is
filled with swirls of incense smoke.

In all there are about 800,000 monks in
Burma, of whom over 100,000 are lifelong members, the rest spending varying
times in the order (*sangha*) which they can
leave at any time. Many young Burmese
men spend the three-month rainy season
each summer in a monastery, thereby
bringing spiritual merit not only to
themselves, but to their family, especially
their mother. Novices are accepted from
the age of about nine, the minimum age at
which one can become a full-time monk
being twenty. A novice not only gains a
good education, but has the opportunity to
make contacts that will stand him in good
stead should he decide to leave the order.

The *sangha* has a unique role in Burma,
with many of its senior members involved
in the government in an uneasy alliance
with the military. Modern life has softened
monastic discipline: today's *pongyi* may
well have a taste for the local cheroots and
will probably know all about the Internet.
But there are still retreat centres and rural
communities like Sagaing, where life is
dedicated to an austere routine of long
hours of daily meditation and scriptural
study; possessions are limited to a wooden
alms bowl, three sets of robes, a razor,
needle-and-cotton and a water-filter.

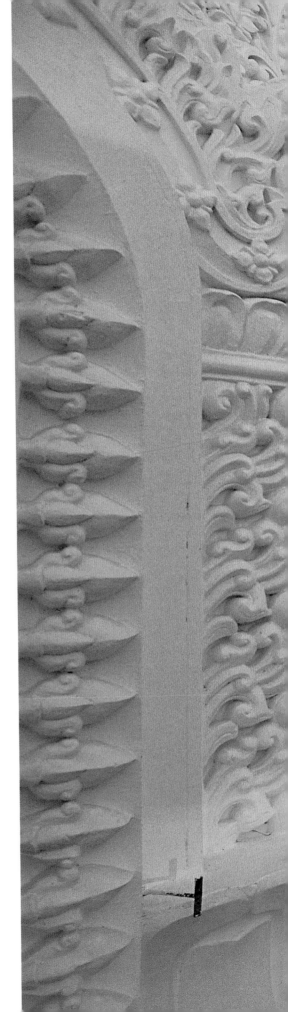

Si Satchanalai, Thailand
King Ramkamhaeng's Citadel

IF YOU FOLLOW THE CHAO PHRYA river north from Bangkok through the lush irrigated central plains that are Thailand's rice bowl, you will come across a deserted citadel that lies like a discarded jewel at the heart of the kingdom's history. Si Satchanalai was a regional capital of Sukhothai, hub of the newly formed Thai nation, from the 13th to the 15th century A.D., the highpoint of classical Thai culture. After the decline of the Sukhothai dynasty, the place lay deserted and overgrown until it was put on the map by a retired British Consul called Reginald le May, who fell quite in love with Thailand and devoted himself to exploration. Le May wandered around the country by train, bus, bicycle, elephant, pony and on foot, and wrote as he wandered, correctly surmising in his *Buddhist Art in Siam* that Si Satchanalai's Wat Chang Lom, a pivotal monument built of volcanic laterite bricks stuccoed and painted, owed its elephant buttressing to Singalese influence.

'In the water there are fish,
in the paddies rice.
The lord of the land does not raise taxes
from his people taking cattle
over his fields or horses over his lands.
Those who want to play, play.
Those who want to sing, sing.
Those who want to laugh, laugh.'

STELE OF KING RAMKAMHAENG

LEFT The evocative ruins of Si Satchanalai: an image of the Buddha seated on the serpent king, Muchalinda; the main *prang* of Wat Mahathat, Chalieng, is in the background.

King Ramkamhaeng's Citadel

Ramkamhaeng, first king of the united Thai nation, summoned monks from Ceylon who brought not only Pali scriptures, but architectural ideas and iconographical rules to inspire the Theravada Buddhism that has remained Thailand's official religion to this day. As his stele, carved in 1292, proudly announces, the king built 'the elephant-girded *chedi*' (the Thai word for *stupa*) in 1285 to house relics of the Buddha. With its stairway mimicking a ladder to heaven, its two terraces as artificial mountains linking the mundane to the celestial and its bell-shaped spire signifying enlightenment, Wat Chang Lom was the prototype of hundreds of *chedis* that were to follow, their domes swelling like spiritual breasts to nourish the faithful.

The most important monument here, Wat Chedi Chet Taew, is modelled on Wat Mahathat, 'the Monastery of the Great Relic', in neighbouring Sukhothai: a group of buildings – *chedis*, colonnaded assembly halls, chapels – aligned on an east-west axis to the rising sun and centred on the Khmer-style central tower (*prang*). Its harmonious dignity still evident, the site was meant to demonstrate the ordering power of cosmic intelligence, with the *prang*'s elegant 'lotus bud' finial, unique to the Sukhothai style, symbolizing the purity of the Buddha's doctrine. Surrounding this soaring central feature are other *chedis* in a variety of styles; many contain the ashes of the princes who once ruled Si Satchanalai.

ABOVE AND RIGHT
The summit of Wat Mahathat's tower, its finial crowned with five sacred parasols and the flag of the *dharma*; a view across the walled enclosure of Wat Chedi Taew to the lotus-bud tower.

Wat Phra Kaeo, Thailand
Emerald Buddha Temple

IN 1767, AYUTTHAYA, the royal capital of the Thais, was sacked by their old enemy, the Burmese. The defeated Thai nation, under their king, Taksin, struggled fifty miles downriver to the Gulf of Siam, to regroup at a small fishing village known as Bang Kok, 'the village of the wild plums', which since the middle of the century had been Ayutthaya's main port. Bang Kok was an open door to foreign trade, especially the shipment of arms, and with stout fortifications built by the French was safe from the Burmese to the north and west. But Taksin was not to see the founding of a new kingdom. Exhausted by years of military campaigning, he became increasingly unstable, prey to delusions of grandeur and paranoia, torturing his officials, wife and children.

In March 1782 a revolt broke out, the mad king fled to a monastery, and the throne was offered to the commander of his forces, a general named Chao Phya Chakri. Taking the name Rama I, the new king inaugurated the Chakri dynasty, which rules Thailand to this day. The hapless Taksin was disposed of in a manner suitable for royalty, whose blood should never touch the ground. After a performance of sacred dance and music had sanctified the scene, he was wrapped in a black velvet sack and his neck deftly broken with a club of delicately scented sandalwood.

Rama's first concern in establishing his new capital was to build a temple to house the Emerald Buddha, an image he had captured during a military expedition in Laos some months before. Much of his popularity was due to his association with this sacred talisman, believed to have great magical powers. The temple, Wat Phra Kaeo, was set on the east bank of the Chao Phrya river, and the king lived in a wooden hut on the site until it was completed. Only then did he have his Grand Palace built adjacent to it. Known as the Emerald Buddha temple, Wat Phra Kaeo is the the most revered site in the kingdom, and although the king's personal chapel, it is open to the public daily.

Entering the white walled compound the visitor is met with a dazzling and closely packed display of brilliantly embellished buildings, a riot of colour spread over hard gilded surfaces and ceramic

'One who practises to develop the heart is one who practises Buddhism.'

AJAHN CHAH, THAI MEDITATION MASTER

OPPOSITE AND THIS PAGE
The Emerald Buddha temple complex: the Phra Si Ratana Chedi, the Mondop and the Prasat Phra Thepidon; applying gold leaf in the Chao Mae Guan enclosure; the Emerald Buddha in rainy season robes; meetings in the compound.

Emerald Buddha Temple

ABOVE AND OPPOSITE
Views of Wat Phra
Kaeo: the north porch
of Prasat Phra Thep
Bidorn; a gilded
Buddha figure in
sumptuous courtly
dress; a magnificent
kinnara – half-bird,
half-man – guards the
shrine.

and mirrored tile-work. This is an art of sumptuous decoration, a polychrome aesthetic that clothes the sacred in layer upon glittering layer, expressing adoration through a process of unrestrained yet somehow unfussy accumulation. Here the Thai love of brilliance meets the doctrine of the temple as the earthly palace of the gods – an idea inherited from the ancient Khmer kingdoms of Hindu Cambodia. The result is a world imbued with magical influences, heavy with the sweet scent of jasmine and sandalwood joss-sticks, tinkling with the sound of wind-chimes, their clappers delicately shaped like the leaf of the *bodhi* tree. Inlaid pavilions and fluttering pigeons, bells, candles and offering bowls, pinks, greens, yellows and blues all mingle together, set off by the unclouded blue of the sky and the deep orange of monastic robes. Happy, thoughtless children skip around, and everywhere smiling people enjoying that most vital ingredient of Thai life, *sanuk* – 'good fun' – for although religion is a very serious business in Thailand, it is never too solemn.

As one approaches the temple, three of the kingdom's most important buildings are seen next to each other on a platform. First to catch the eye is a gleaming gold dome with ringed spire, nostalgically modelled on those at the royal chapel in Ayutthaya. Next to this stands a square pavilion (*mondop*) topped by an elegant spire ascending in tiers. In most temples the *mondop* houses a Buddha image or relic; here it was built as a library to hold the *Tripitika*, the sacred scriptures of Buddhism, which repose in a mother-of-pearl casket within.

Lastly, covered in blue and red tiles, comes the royal pantheon building, Phra Thepidon, which contains the lifesize statues of the first eight kings of the Chakri dynasty. Gilded capitals and carved gilded gables sweep up to an elegant spire (*prang*), another legacy of the Khmers. Guarding the building stand gilded *kinnaras*: half-human, half-bird, eloquently symbolizing the spiritual aspirations of Thai art. Everything here soars upwards – spires, finials, slender columns, curved eaves and roof peaks – expressing the hierarchy of perfection.

All of this is but a preparation for the Emerald Buddha, housed in a lofty hall (*bot*), whose walls, peopled with murals of deities, Buddhas and royal court scenes, rise sixty feet to a ceiling of red and dull gold. Perhaps a hundred worshippers sit silently on the floor, legs tucked under them, absorbing the presence. Sanctity is compounded by remoteness: the Emerald Buddha is only about thirty inches high, sitting nearly forty feet up on banked tiers of gold platforms like some imperious child god, ensconced in a glass cabinet tapering away to a gold finial and flanked by the sacred nine-tier parasols. The foreign visitor may initially be disappointed: the image is too small to be seen clearly, not even emerald but a type of green jasper. Photography is strictly forbidden. But there is something special here if you let the mind settle and absorb the atmosphere. So much respect has been afforded this small object over the years; even today, at the start of each new season, the king carefully wraps its shoulders with a new robe: gold and diamond for the summer, gold flecked with blue for the rainy season, and one of heavy gold chain encased in enamel to keep it warm during the cold season. The Emerald Buddha is an icon put to its most influential purpose, as strength concentrated in the subtle energy of the seed, the taming power of the small. This tiny statue holds court over high and low alike, united in their reverential awe. This alone is a type of magic.

ABOVE AND RIGHT
The bell-tower and gable of the Sala Rai shrine; the Chedi, Mondop and Phra Thep Bidorn from the west portico of the Ubosot.

THE GREAT
Mahayana Buddhism

SOMETIME AROUND the beginning of the Christian era, a group of
Buddhist schools emerged with a radical reinterpretation of the *dharma*.
They argued that the Buddha's message had become distorted by the
Theravada's dry scholasticism, reclusive austerity and disparaging
dismissals of everyday life. Calling itself the Mahayana ('Great Vehicle'),
this group dubbed the Theravadins the Hinayana ('Little Vehicle'),
implying that, by following the new teachings, everybody could tread the
path to *nirvana*. Whereas early Buddhism was a discipline suitable only to
the monk, whose goal was subjective freedom from impermanence and

suffering, the Mahayana emphasized compassion for all living beings,
whatever their abilities. It expanded the experience of *nirvana* to include
the objective world, and taught that all life was a manifestation of a
blissful and universal 'buddha nature', inherent in everything.
This new vision revitalized Buddhism, transforming it into a popular
religion. A celestial pantheon was created, peopled with myriad beings in
countless universes, including hierarchies of celestial Buddhas and their
consorts. Ritual and worship expanded to serve these deities, and while
the historical Buddha came to be seen increasingly as a saviour, a new

VEHICLE
from the Himalayas to Japan

type of being, the *bodhisattva* ('pure-minded one') was celebrated as an exemplary figure who, selflessly unconcerned with his personal enlightenment, teaches the *dharma* to all. Ironically, as time progressed the Mahayana became increasingly like the Hinduism the Master had originally rejected, recasting truths in a form suitable to the times.

The Mahayana expansion of doctrine was accompanied by an explosion of artistic creativity. Sculptures in stone and bronze were created in vast numbers, the monumental reliquary (*stupa*) of the Theravadins became much more ornate and symbolic, and mural painting thrived in new

forms. One of these, the *mandala*, a geometric map of the cosmos used as a meditational aid, became a particularly succinct and accomplished encapsulation of the teachings.

Whereas the Theravada had flourished throughout south-east Asia, the Mahayana initially took a northern route, reaching central Asia (*c.* A.D. 20), China (*c.* A.D. 65) and Japan (*c.* A.D. 500), and then spreading into the Himalayan kingdoms of Nepal (*c.* A.D. 400) and Tibet (*c.* A.D. 625). It has given birth to some of the world's most powerful spiritual teachings and greatest cultural treasures.

Borobodur, Java
The Cosmic Mandala

I
T IS HARD TO IMAGINE a place more blessed than the Kedu valley of central Java. Surrounded by protective mountains, glittering emerald paddy-fields and tasselled palm groves spring from the rich volcanic soil which, watered by regular rainfall, grants several bountiful rice harvests a year. Historically, this plain must always have been relatively densely populated; its sacred nature is evinced by the fact that within the central five kilometres, the remains of over thirty Hindu temples have been unearthed. As the geographical hub of the island, the valley was considered its *brahmasthan*, that point in the material world at which the nourishing cosmic energies are most potently manifest. Little wonder it was here that the Javanese chose to build, roughly between A.D. 780-830, what is perhaps the most remarkable sacred structure in Asia: the cosmic mandala of Borobodur.

Historical records are sparse. We know the central authority at the time was the Shailendra dynasty, followers of the Mahayana Buddhism then galvanizing south and south-east Asia, and we know they were in contact with great Buddhist centres in India. Borobodur sculpture is influenced by the contemporary Pala-Sena school found in Bengal. But we do not know the details of Borobodur – the names of its royal patron, its architects or builders, the numbers of labourers, the time they took to create such a marvel. Records do infer they were not, as is often assumed, slave labourers. The intermittent pattern of labour needed for rice cultivation freed workers for long periods each year, during which they often worked on religious monuments out of respect for kings they felt had ruled well. Such projects embodied the collective consciousness – rich and poor, monk and lay person – in its perennial and shared task of aligning human society to the Divine.

Borobodur has long puzzled western experts. Usually called a *stupa*, its crowning dome is actually far too small in relation to the supporting mass to be a *stupa* as normally understood, yet the scale and ubiquitously fine carving show it was clearly a site of superlative importance. The unconventional proportions caused Albert Foucher, the nineteenth-century scholar, to sniff, 'It resembles a badly risen cake'. Fifty years later Paul Mus first proposed that Borobodur was perhaps just what it looked like: a *stupa* set atop a vast stepped pyramid of a base. This base was probably built by Hindus as the foundation of a gigantic pyramidal temple; then, under the wave of Buddhist fervour that swept Java around A.D. 790, new builders took over, converting the structure to their faith. The result is a unique whole combining the supreme emblem of the Buddhist *dharma* in its newly expanded Mahayana form, with the stepped mountain, ancient symbol of the abode of the ancestors. Hence the name Borobodur, a colloquial shortening of the Sanskrit *bhumisambharabhudara,* meaning 'The Mountain of Virtues of the Ten Stages of the Bodhisattva's Path'.

Virtue aside, the sheer hard work needed to construct this magic mountain was extraordinary. Over 1,600,000 blocks of andesite stone were hauled from the valley's river beds to be cut and dressed for the base, while more skilled hands painstakingly fashioned 500 large

OPPOSITE AND THIS PAGE
Latticed *stupas,* containing *dhyani* Buddha images, on the three uppermost terraces; inside a *stupa*; a compassionate *bodhisattva*; a patron of the *sangha* offers alms to a *bodhisattva*.

The Cosmic Mandala

Buddha statues and over 1,500 relief panels, many as large as 275 x 100 cms., which run in eleven rows around the monument, totalling a length of well over 3,000 metres.

But it is in its symbolic message that Borobodur is perhaps boldest, and certainly most complex. Composed of five ascending square terraces leading to three circular ones around a central crowning *stupa*, this enormous squared circle constitutes nothing less than a map of the cosmos. As is most clearly visible from

ABOVE AND OPPOSITE
The peace of the Buddha expressed in a carved head with the 'third eye' of wisdom in the centre of the forehead; monumental statuary decorates the balustrade wall on the second terrace.

aerial photographs, it is a vast and three-dimensional stone *mandala*, depicting the hierarchical levels of material reality that emanate from, and return to, the radiant divine Consciousness the Mahayana calls 'The Unboundedness' (*shunyata*). For the pilgrim, to circumambulate and ascend this mountain-*stupa* is symbolically to transcend the realms of matter and, transfigured by the apotheosis of the summit, to return, re-born, to a new life in the world. As such, it stands as a physical analogue of both the Buddhist's daily practice of meditation and his lifelong pilgrimage.

The base of the monument is largely hidden from view, probably shored up by earth not long after its construction due to the structure's instability. But we know its carved panels depict everyday scenes of life as portrayed in a popular text the *Karmavibhangga Sutra*, and represent, 'the world of desire' (*kamadhatu*), the typical human life where people are driven by their cravings.

The first-floor panels are devoted to the exemplary story of the life of the historical Buddha, Shakyamuni, as described in another important Mahayana scripture, the *Lalitavistara Sutra*, as well as homilies and parables, and stories from his previous lives (*jatakas*). The latter continue to the second gallery. From there, and continuing on through the galleries of the third and fourth terraces, another seminal text, the *Gandavyuha Sutra*, is illustrated. This tells the story of Sudhana, an Everyman figure, and his long and testing wanderings in search of spiritual Enlightenment. In the final series of reliefs, Sudhana is taught meditation by the *bodhisattva* Samatabhadra, Conveyor of Perfect Wisdom, and eventually achieves *nirvana*. The sinuous beauty of these panels, overlooked by meditating Buddhas, regularly spaced in 432 niches of

the balustrade above, is a fine example of the spiritualized sensuality of the best Buddhist art. All these terraces, introverted and overhung, represent the 'world of forms' (*rupadhatu*), which are subtler than the *kamadhatu*, and in which we are progressively free of desire but still bound by our limited individuality.

Next come three round terraces set with 72 latticed *stupas* which were probably covered in gold leaf. The *stupas*, in three decreasing concentric circles of 32, 24 and 16, are multiples of an essential 8 – the holy Buddhist number we have already met in the eight terraces – symbolizing the Eightfold Noble Path of Buddhism. The other number which, in various symbolic combinations, occurs throughout the site is 9: the 432 gallery statues, for example, total 9 [4+3+2] and are multiples of it, [7x8x9]. The fretted *stupas* combine these two numbers, 72 being 8x9. Each *stupa* contains, half-hidden behind his cage of stone, a *dhyani* Buddha, one of the Mahayana's five celestial Buddhas who symbolize the five cardinal directions, the five great elements and the five great qualities. These beings float half-way between the seen and the unseen, linking our material world to the world of pure spirit, hence their fugitive presence behind their fretted screens. These three terraces represent 'the world without forms' (*arupadhatu*), where the mind is free from identification with the transient phenomenal world.

At the summit stands a single crowning *stupa*. Empty under the sky, it symbolizes the level of life that is beyond any personalized limitation, the transcendent Void (*shunyata*), source and goal of all.

Abandoned when Islam overran Java in the fifteenth century, the monument remained virtually forgotten for centuries. Then, in 1815, Stamford Raffles, British representative in Java, discovered the

overgrown and delapidated site, became
entranced by it and had it cleared. It was
he who introduced Borobodur to the
western world in his *History of Java*
[1844]. The following year Adolf Schaefer
took the first photographs of the site. Theo
van Erp attempted valuable restoration
work from 1905-11, but before long
damaging cracks due to water seepage
threatened the monument again. A long
period of indecision followed, not least
because obtaining government funds in
Islamic Java for a Buddhist monument
was no easy business. Finally, in 1973, an
enormous and complete restoration
scheme was begun by UNESCO. The square
terraces were totally dismantled, each
piece of stone cleaned and treated with
fungicide; reinforced concrete foundations
with drainage channels were installed, and
the whole was reassembled. Thanks to
extraordinary international cooperation,
the cosmic *mandala* was again restored to
its resplendent glory.

LEFT AND ABOVE
An exposed figure of
the Buddha looks out
serenely over the valley
from the summit of
Borobodur; the temple
complex seen from the
south.

Angkor Thom and Banteay Chhmar, Cambodia
Buddha Kings of the Khmer

THE LAST GREAT BUILDER of the sumptuous Khmer civilization was Jayavarman VII [A.D. 1181–1220]. In 1177, Angkor was sacked by the neighbouring kingdom of Cham; it took Jayavarman, then aged fifty and with no experience of ruling, four years of battle on land and water to defeat them. Victorious, he immediately undertook an energetic programme of rebuilding. Rejecting Angkor's traditional defences of wooden ramparts, he built more than twenty-two miles of massive sandstone walls around the site, and filled it with dozens of religious buildings. There followed no less than 102 hospitals, an extensive arterial road system served by 121 travellers' rest-houses, and the restoration and enlargement of the network of waterways on which the Khmer had always depended.

An ardent Mahayanist, Jayavarman lost no time in rooting the family tree securely in heaven. The earliest of his major monuments, Ta Prohm, was a shrine dedicated to his mother as Prajnaparamita, the Mahayana goddess of transcendental wisdom. It housed 260 precious images, and its monastery, so an inscription tells us, was supported by 3,000 villages and almost 80,000 people. Among its treasures were over 500 kilos of golden dishes, and large quantities of jewels, Chinese silk and inlaid woodwork.

Next came Preah Khan dedicated to his father, regarded as an incarnation of Lokeshvara, deity of compassion. Its sandstone buildings are embellished by exquisite carving, their interior walls undulating with the graceful forms of Buddhist deities, vast battle scenes and Sanskrit epigraphy in elegant Khmer script. But the classical regularity of Angkor Wat's five towers was abandoned and as the complex was frequently, and almost haphazardly, added to during the forty years of Jayavarman's reign, the final effect is somewhat confused.

Angkor Thom, 'the Large City', was the new royal capital, built not far north of Suryavarman's Angkor Wat. Like its predecessor, Angkor Thom was surrounded by a moat. The bridges, flanked by gods and demons pulling on the cosmic serpent Sheshanaga, dramatize the episode from Indian myth when the powers of heaven and hell engaged in a mighty tug-of-war, churning the Cosmic Ocean to produce the elixir of immortality.

The geographic and mystical centre of Angkor Thom was the Bayon, a huge pyramidal temple with over 50 towers, dedicated to the Buddha, with whom Jayavarman identified himself. This adroit alignment substituted the concept of *buddharaja*, King as Buddha, for the earlier *devaraja* cult. Such aggrandisement was apparently contagious; twelve subsidiary chapels surround the centre, each housing the image of a deified regional governor. The Bayon towers are carved with a motif that has become the hallmark of Buddhist Angkor, a series of magnificent heads, found also on the site's imposing entrance gateways and many of its other shrines. The almond eyes, broad brow and cheeks, and wide nose are recognizably Cambodian, yet they radiate a delicate and spiritual fullness that is hardly of this world. These heads probably represent Lokeshvara, and thus the king; indeed, it may be that they are actually portraits of Jayavarman. This possibility, together with his relentless building and rebuilding (though many of his monuments were structurally weakened by the haste of their construction) have led historians to speculate that the king was a megalomaniac, a conclusion that could be dismissed or confirmed by the fulsome praises heaped on him in contemporary inscriptions.

The pattern now established was to continue at Banteay Chhmar, 'The Narrow Fortress', in Cambodia's extreme north-west. Relatively

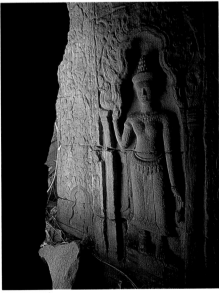

OPPOSITE AND THIS PAGE One of the Bayon's giant heads of Lokeshvara, thought to be that of Jayavarman VII; a nun offering incense at Tep Pranam, Angkor Thom; a bas-relief of a goddess in a gallery of Preah Khan.

isolated, the citadel boasts a wealth of bas-reliefs that are as fine as those of the better-known buildings at Angkor Thom.

Repeated invasions by the Thais gradually whittled away the power of a state increasingly exhausted by the heavy taxes, frenetic building programmes and lengthy wars needed to maintain its autocratic rulers. By the middle of the sixteenth century the Khmers abandoned Angkor, with its brocaded silks, firework displays and sumptuous dance shows, and retreated south and east to build a more modest capital at Phnom Penh. An era uniquely lavish in its aspirations, achievements and pageantry had come to an end, leaving the voracious jungle to take over once more.

ABOVE AND OPPOSITE
Devata in a gallery in
Ta Prohm; a face tower
in the style of the
Bayon in the remains of
Banteay Chhmar.

Swayambhunath, Nepal
The Lotus-born Stupa

LONG, LONG AGO, when even the gods were young, there was a remote Himalayan valley filled with a turquoise lake whose crystalline waters were so pure they reflected the surrounding snowy peaks without a single blemish. In the middle of this lake floated a wondrous thousand-petalled lotus. The gleaming golden flower radiated a pellucid blue light – the infinite Buddha nature that illumines all creation – which drew seekers from all the known world to come to live and meditate on the shores of the lake. News of the wonder reached China and the mighty *bodhisattva* Manjushri, Lord of Wisdom, who dwelt there on the splendorous Five-peaked Mountain. Arriving at the lake, Manjushri was filled with the desire to worship the lotus more closely and to bring its benefits to all sentient beings. Drawing his razor-sharp sword of discrimination, he sliced the lake in two. The water drained out, and at the point where the lotus settled on the valley floor he built a huge mound – the shrine now known as Swayambhunath, 'the Self-created Lord' – to support it for evermore. Encircling the magical mound with a fertile plain, Manjushri founded a city, Manjupattan, and appointed his purest devotee as its king. He also instructed the people in agriculture and craftsmanship and taught them the Ten Rites of Passage which would keep them aligned with the Natural Law that governs all life.

So runs the Nepalese legend on the founding of the *stupa* whose tall golden spire overlooks the Kathmandu valley from a grassy hill west of the city. As the *bindu* ('seed point') from which the universe was born, the mysterious transition between non-existence and existence, Swayambhunath is the centre of the magical *Nepali mandala*, what the outside world calls the Kathmandu Valley.

Though archaeological remains in the valley only go back two thousand years to the time of the Mongoloid Kirata people,

> *'This self-created temple of wisdom*
> *confers spiritual liberation*
> *by seeing it, by touching it,*
> *by hearing of it, or by reflecting on it.'*
>
> NEWARI CHRONICLE

LEFT A young monk studies sacred texts on the balcony of a *gompa*, in the Swayambhunath complex.

The Lotus-born Stupa

and the history of the shrine itself is traced from an inscription of A.D. 460, its commandingly elevated site must have been the spiritual focus of the valley since the dawn of civilization here. No doubt it served the various layers of Nepalese religious belief – animistic, mother goddess worship, devotion to Shiva and Vishnu – which all preceded, and then intermingled with, the most recent stratum, Buddhism.

Swayambhunath figures at all important moments of Nepalese history. We know that the first king of the Licchavi dynasty had his cremation rites performed here in the fifth century, that the great *guru* Padmasambhava, who took the *dharma* to Tibet, visited it some three hundred years later, establishing Yama, the Black Lord of Death, as its protector, and that it then became a renowned centre of the *tantric* teachings for which the valley has long

been famous. In 1346, Muslim invaders from Bengal tried in vain to destroy the *stupa*; it survived to rise again, assuming its present form in the mid seventeenth century.

Climbing a long stairway flanked by fabulous guardian creatures and surrounded by trees, the visitor emerges on to a plateau that, like many Nepalese shrines, initially seems more of a farmyard than a temple. Chattering monkeys, chickens and dogs run freely, chased by tiny children through scattered offerings of flowers and food and the fragrant woody smoke of juniper incense. Rice flecked with bright red – blood and earth, the ubiquitous colour of the goddess – crunches under the feet. As befits the easy tolerance of the Nepalese, the place is a jumble of different structures, many covered in superb gilded copper repoussé. There is the shrine dedicated to the fierce deities Bhairava and Bhairavi, whose basement contains many weapons; the temples to the five elements; the House of the Secret God, believed to be the abode of the *nagas*, the serpent kings and queens. Particularly striking is the Drukpa Kargu Buddhist monastery on the west of the platform, founded by the Bhutanese royal family; most popular is the shrine to Shitala, 'the Cooling One', who guards children and protects them from illness – smallpox in particular. Each Saturday her shrine is thronged by Newari women, their long black hair braided with brilliant red tresses, babies slung on their hips.

The calm axis of this swirl of human activity is the *stupa's* golden spire, its thirteen rings representing the stages on the path to Enlightenment. Crowning it is a parasol, an ancient symbol of royalty, alluding in the Buddhist context both to Gautama's royal upbringing and, by its shape, to the *bodhi* tree under which he attained *nirvana*, the truly regal state.

ABOVE AND RIGHT
The evening circumambulation of the *stupa*; the tiers of the spire represent stages of the way to *nirvana*. Buddhas look out over the four directions from its base.

Bodhnath, Nepal
The All-seeing Buddha

S O DEEP is the sonorous chanting that at first it sounds more like the rhythmic undulation of some elemental force than the product of the human voice. Only after some time does it become apparent that this ebb and flow of primordial sound emanates from a burgundy-robed group of monks sitting in the shadow of the strangely futuristic dome, as much like a spaceship as an ancient Buddhist shrine, that is the great *stupa* of Bodhnath: 'the Lord of Enlightenment'. Next to the monks is a small temple-shrine whose grille conceals a silver image of 'Grandmother' Ajima, otherwise known as Pukashi, the protectress of the cremation ground. She is shown devouring the entrails of a corpse. It is appropriate that this fearsome Hindu deity is worshipped by Tibetans as Jadzimo, the humble female devotee who built the *stupa*, for the site is named in Tibetan *tantric* texts as being one of the eight great cremation grounds of the Buddhist world, a place where all the

'*Whoever offers music to the Great Stupa spreads the vibration of the* dharma *throughout the ten directions; whoever offers the sound of cymbals obtains deep and strong understanding and prosperity; whoever offers the sound of tinkling bells obtains a sweet and gentle voice.*'

THE LEGEND OF THE GREAT STUPA

LEFT AND RIGHT Ritual prostration to the great *stupa*; the all-seeing eyes of the Buddha symbolize the universal relevance of the Mahayana teaching.

The All-seeing Buddha

various spirit realms meet together.

Bodhnath is the largest *stupa* in Nepal, and has drawn Buddhist pilgrims from all over the Himalayas, China and Central Asia since its founding around A.D. 500. We know that it was visited by Padmasambhava, who concealed esoteric teachings here in the eighth century to be discovered by future accomplished *yogis*, and that it was restored by Padmasambhava's reincarnation, the great Tibetan miracle-worker Shakya Zangpo, in the fifteenth century. Sketches from nineteenth-century European travellers show that the structure has changed very little in the last hundred years, and since the nineteen-sixties it has been the magnetic centre of a thriving community of Tibetan exiles, whose monasteries, shops and infectious laughter animate the little village that surrounds the dome.

A variation on the general type prevalent in the Kathmandu Valley, the *stupa* is built around a wooden axis (*yasti*) that runs throughout the entire structure, 'linking' it to the heavens. Three tiers of platform (*medhi*) are surmounted by a flattish dome (*anda* or *garbha*) set on a low drum, which is in turn surmounted by a square base (*harmika*) leading to a truncated pyramid of a spire (*kunta*) topped by a fringed parasol (*chattra*) and flame-like finial. When seen from the air the perfectly proportioned whole appears as a three-dimensional *mandala*, conforming to the squared circle as a universal image of perfection. In each side of the square *harmika*, above the number 1 – symbolizing the unity of life – are set the eyes of the Buddha, casting their compassionate gaze out to all corners of the universe, and drawing in all who are alert enough to heed his teaching.

The *stupa* transforms the tumulus of the dead into a source of inspiration for the living. As its name (*anda* = 'egg'; *garbha* = 'womb') implies, the dome contains sacred relics (*bija* = 'seed') to disseminate positive influence into the community. This emanative energy is the cosmic out-breath, enacting the original and continuous creation of the universe from its unmanifest centre. Symbolically the *stupa* images the material universe, unfolding through sequential stages of manifestation from the transcendental through the causal and subtle realms to the gross level of everyday life. This manifestation takes form through the descending hierarchy of the five elements; thus creation first emerges from space (crowning finial), to air (parasol), to fire (spire), to water (dome) and finally down to earth (base). The complementary movement of re-absorption, the cosmic in-breath, conducts the return, through spiritual practice, of the individual to his source in the universal Buddha-nature.

This level of symbolism aligns the ascending components of the structure to the hierarchy of energy centres (*chakras*) in the human nervous system, each of which must be fully purified and enlivened as the physical basis of the state of Enlightenment. The hidden wooden axis alludes to the subtle median nerve in the spinal column, which links the *chakras*.

Such esoteric teachings may be understood and practised in the four active monasteries around the *stupa*, but they probably do not bother the constant flow of simple pilgrims here. These people come for help, reassurance and thanksgiving, obeying an innate religious instinct that we have lost in the West. The greatest celebration of all occurs every twelve years, on the first full moon of the Tibetan Year of the Bird, (the next will fall in 2005), but each year is punctuated with festivals, such as New Year (Vaisaka) – when Buddha's birthday, Enlightenment and death are all rolled into one

celebration – and Ajima's day. These are usually riotous affairs with processions, singing, dancing, and throwing rice to feed the gods.

But even when the religious calendar is empty, everyday devotion never ceases. There are always pilgrims, patiently circumambulating the *stupa* clockwise, telling their rosaries, spinning the copper prayer-wheels, intoning the great mantra OM MANI PEME HUNG, while the deep chanting of the burgundy-robed monks continues unabated...

LEFT AND ABOVE
The skies of late afternoon lower over the great *stupa* of Bodhnath bedecked with cotton prayer-flags; salutations to the *stupa* as centre of the universe.

Samye, Tibet
Buddhism Reaches Tibet

THE FIRST BUDDHIST MONASTERY in Tibet was Samye, founded in A.D. 779 by the great Padmasambhava, the miracle-working adept who brought Buddhism from his home in north-west India. When Guru Rimpoche, 'Precious Teacher' as he is known, arrived here, he encountered the indigenous religion of Bon-po, a type of central Asian shamanism that set great store by psychic experience, oracular trances and communion with spirits. It was the combination of this with his Mahayana message, together with *tantric* teachings from north-east India, that resulted in the esoteric and elaborate form of Buddhism practised in Tibet, known as the Vajrayana, 'the Way of the Adamantine Thunderbolt'. As the beginning of its monastic tradition, Samye is the root and glory of Tibet's religious life. It is laid out, like other Mahayana sanctuaries we have already seen, as an architectural model of the cosmological order, but many of its structures are unique in their design.

As the first monastery of the new faith, Samye took a couple of hundred years to become the seminal centre of political, economic and cultural influence. Over the centuries it has belonged to a succession of the major schools of Tibetan Buddhism – Nyingmapa, Sakhyapa and Gelugpa – and today its monks continue this eclectic tradition, belonging to both the Sakhyapa and Nyingmapa schools. The place has had a turbulent recent history. In 1816, only forty years after a major renovation, it was devastated by an earthquake; ten years later it was badly damaged by fire. During the Cultural Revolution of the nineteen-sixties Red Guards ravaged the monastery. The Utse, its central shrine, had its gold roof ripped off and one floor destroyed, hundreds of *chortens* (the Tibetan form of *stupa*) were razed, thousands of images and ritual implements stolen. Unlike over three thousand temples and monasteries destroyed by the invading Chinese, Samye at least still stands, and the Utse was restored in 1989 due to the efforts of the last Panchen Lama. But the place is suffused with an atmosphere of impermanence, a poignant testimony to the Buddhist teachings on the ephemeral nature of the world. Parts of the complex are still in ruins, and much of the surrounding town has been lost to encroaching dunes, eerily fulfilling Padmasambhava's prediction that his monastery would eventually be buried under sand.

'May I recognize whatever visions appear after death as the reflections of my own consciousness; may I know them to be of the nature of apparitions in the in-between state; at this all-important moment making real progress, may I not fear the peaceful and wrathful deities.'

THE TIBETAN BOOK OF THE DEAD

OPPOSITE AND THIS PAGE The entrance to the main shrine is protected by a white banner with the Wheel of Law; pilgrims worship at the entrance; a visiting monk and acolyte; the quarters of the resident monks.

Buddhism Reaches Tibet

ABOVE AND OPPOSITE
The treasures of the *dharma* crowned by the ceremonial conch shell which dispels negative forces; the great Guru and *tantric* master Padmasambhava, in a chapel of the central Utse shrine.

Standing at the centre of the complex, the Utse is a model of the sacred centre of the universe, Mount Meru. Stepped terraces fronting the halls on each of its three floors give the whole the appearance of an ascending pyramid-mountain. The stone ground floor is designed with traditional Tibetan inward-sloping walls and trapezoid windows; the middle, with its elaborate ceilings and columns, shows Chinese influence, such as is found on Khotamese buildings along the old Silk Route. The crowning third storey, made of wood, is a version of the Indian *mahavihara*: a tiered central building oriented to the cardinal points, topped off with a lotus finial and surrounded by four smaller temples. Though these four have been destroyed, the closeness to the Indian model is clear and nowhere near as pronounced elsewhere in Tibet. From this absolute centre lie nested circles of shrines, representing successive levels of the universe radiating out in increasing density.

Surrounded by two walls with gates at the cardinal points, the Utse has its main entrance and its assembly hall (*dukhang*) both facing east to absorb the life energy of the rising sun. Entering the hall, it takes the eye a moment to adjust to a vaporous, dreamlike world: a shadowed, cavernous chamber supported by huge pillars hung with richly brocaded banners. Everywhere is darkened by centuries of smoke from yak-butter lamps; some are three feet across, illuminating dull-glowing vessels of bronze and copper, gold and silver bowls, goblets studded with huge lumps of coral and turquoise and polychrome offerings (*tormas*) sculpted out of butter and flour. The greasy smell of butter mixes with woody juniper incense. Patinated by ephemeral universes of gods and demons, Buddhas and *bodhisattvas*, the walls are also hung with an assembly of spectral presences: intricate paintings mounted on silk (*thankas*) showing lineages of teachers and celestial protectors. The seraphic countenances of peaceful deities smile dreamily alongside the contorted grimaces of their wrathful counterparts, while statues of past spiritual luminaries look down on the worshippers: Guru Rimpoche, Tsong Khapa, founder of the 'Yellow Hat' school, and other scholars and patriarchs.

Between the assembly hall and the inner sanctum stand three magnificent gateways, the Three Doors of Liberation. These symbolize important Mahayanist triads: the Three Marks of Impermanence (old age, illness and death) that afflict all life; the Three Jewels of Buddhism (the Buddha, his teaching and the community of monks) that redeem it; and the Three Subjective Aspects (body, speech and mind), whose complete purification is Enlightenment. Thus the core of the complex, symbolically the infinite source of the universe, is approached through a threshold that represents the human predicament, its remedy and the practical means to achieve it.

The inner sanctum itself, the Jowo Khang, a spiritual fortress surrounded by stone walls over six feet thick, has a passage allowing the pilgrim to circumambulate clockwise under the gaze of the Buddha in his last and previous lives. The gaze is drawn to the magnificent ceiling containing a thousand Buddhas and supported by ten pillars – symbolizing the ten directions – each with eight sides, one for each of the stages of the Eightfold Noble Path. The heart of the shrine is again the trinity of Three Jewels, in the form of a large image of Shakyamuni, the historical Buddha, behind which are huge stacks of the sacred texts, and a throne for the Dalai Lama.

As every part of the complex serves as a vehicle for an aspect of the Mahayana

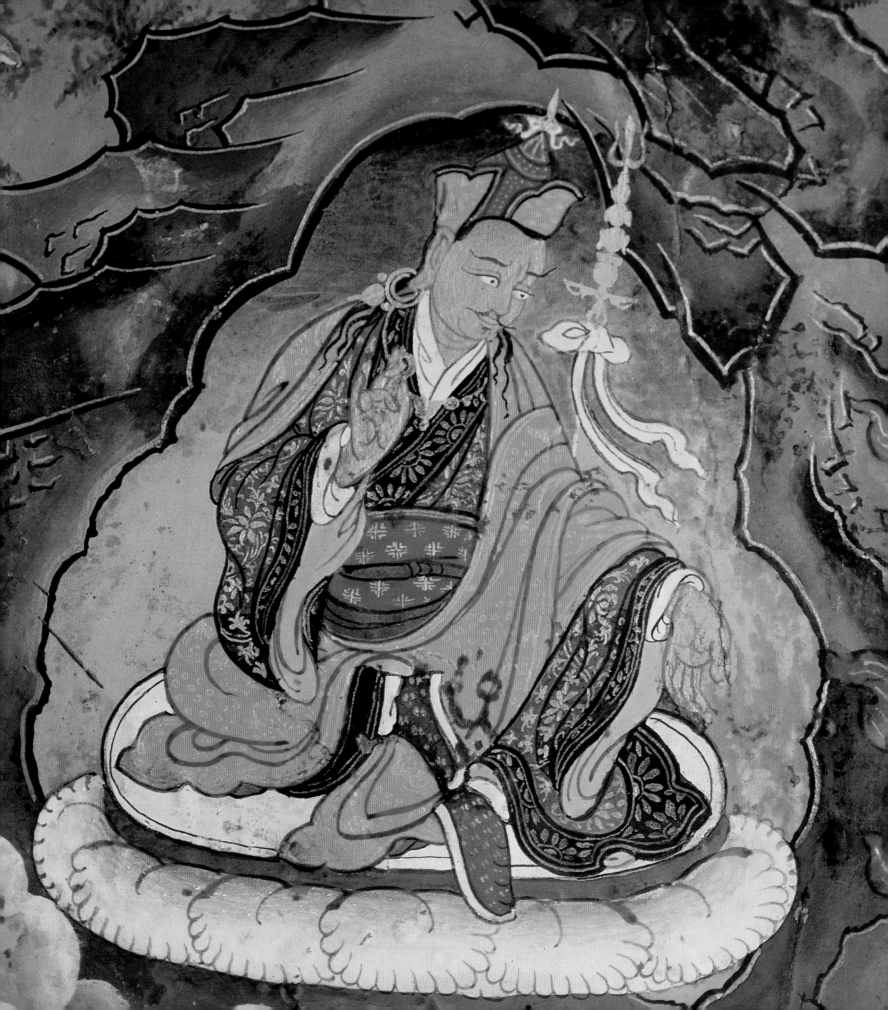

teaching, so the raw energies of the world, in all their primal and terrifying power, are fully acknowledged in the Tibetan pantheon, and each monastery has its dark temple (*gokhang*) dedicated to them. The *gokhang* here is a claustrophic, downright spooky place, full of foreboding. Hung with black *thankas* etched in gold, and filled with stuffed animals and weapons, it is the reception hall for the fearsome deities whose job it is to absorb negative energies and transmute them, thus protecting us. The main deity here, made by Padmasambhava himself, is so fierce, it is said, that anyone unqualified who unveils it will die immediately.

ABOVE AND RIGHT
A *lama* specializing in healing and exorcism rituals; monks chant beneath banners proclaiming the victory of the *dharma*.

Tashilunpo, Tibet
Seat of the Panchen Lamas

NESTLING UNDER THE HILLS of Drolma Ri, outside Shigatse, Tibet's second largest city, lies a sprawling warren of shadowed alleyways and mysterious enclosed courtyards. This is Tashilunpo, the country's largest and most vibrant monastery, with 800 resident monks. It was founded in 1447, by the first Dalai Lama, to be one of the Six Jewels, the great monasteries created as spiritual lighthouses through Tibet to spread the teachings of the great reformer Tsong Khapa, [A.D. 1357-1419] the founder of the Gelugpa 'virtuous ones', known as the 'Yellow Hat' school after their ceremonial headgear. The Gelugpas favoured the moral and philosophical roots of Tibetan Buddhism, rather than its mystical and esoteric practices; contesting the moral laxity of the day, they taught a system that laid great emphasis on textual learning and intellectual training. The reincarnating head of the 'Yellow Hat' school is the best known of all Tibetan Buddhists, the Dalai Lama.

The particular importance of Tashilunpo resides in the fact that its senior monks, the Panchen Lamas, form a reincarnating lineage alongside that of the Dalai Lamas, whom they traditionally recognize and tutor. When the Chinese invaded Tibet in 1959, the tenth Panchen was taken to Beijing. He wrote a highly critical account of the Chinese presence in his homeland, entitled *The 70,000 Characters*, which was only made public in 1997. Finally allowed to return to Tashilunpo in 1988 to conduct a particularly important ceremony, he and both his parents were poisoned during their visit. The present incarnation, a young boy recognized by the Dalai Lama in 1991, is believed to be still alive under detention somewhere in Beijing, while the Chinese have put up their own candidate for the position.

Tashilunpo became a great centre of pilgrimage and a patron of the arts from the mid seventeenth century, when Tibet was united under the fifth Dalai Lama and the Gelugpas dominated the country. At the western end of the elongated complex the Jamkhang Chenmo, a tall red building surmounted by a glittering gold roof, is one huge hall containing an eighty-foot-high image of Maitreya, Buddha of the Future, who in popular belief will be our saviour from the present dark age. Made of gilded bronze and heavily jewelled, this colossus is built up around the trunk of a juniper, a tree held sacred by the Tibetans.

'*This world is impermanent, like a city of illusion.*
It will not last long but is subject to destruction and change.'

GURU PADMASAMBHAVA

OPPOSITE AND THIS PAGE
Ritual prostration around the Groashin *chorten*; the threshold of the shrine; the largest bronze Buddha image in the world, in the Jamkhang Chenmo; the gilded roofs of the Kudhung Lhakhang.

ABOVE AND OPPOSITE
Lighting yak-butter
lamps to be placed
before Buddha images;
free time on the steps
of the Kudhung
Lhakhang.

Seat of the Panchen Lamas

Huge quantities of gold, copper and brass were used for its construction; the figure is filled with relics, magically empowered texts and gold. The heart of the complex is the Palace of the Panchen Lamas, known as the Labrang Gyaltsen Thonpo or 'Palace of the Glorious Victory Banners'. Here tall white walls enclose a building protected on the south by seven interconnected chapels, filled with small bronzes, fine scroll paintings (*thankas*) and complete sets of the scriptures (*kangyur*). This was the residence of the first senior monk, Gedundrub, who had a vision of eleven victory banners on the roof, telling him that eleven successive Panchens would govern the place.

East of the palace lies the Kudhung Lakhang, a large building crowned with a gold roof, whose dull red walls contain the tomb of the fourth Panchen Lama, an ornate silver and gold *chorten* standing forty feet high and dating from 1662. Tibetans often place parts of the corpse of a high lama into such tombs to act as a power-relic, but this tomb is unusual in that the entire body was placed standing up, along with ancient texts and sets of embroidered *thankas* donated by the Manchu emperors of China. The walls are hung with sumptuous brocade and silk in reds, gold, yellows and blues, while a thousand Buddhas look down serenely from their celestial paradise.

At the eastern end of Tashilunpo lies its largest group of buildings, the Kesang Lakhang, a cluster of temples enclosing a large central courtyard. This open space is the sacred centre of Tashilunpo, where its great seasonal festivals are performed with their stately masked dances to purify the environment of negative energies, and the many complex daily rituals through which the life of the monastery is structured and the continued welfare of the universe ensured. An elevated stage provides the eating area for the senior monks and dignitaries, while at the centre of the yard stands a flagpole: the victory banner of the *dharma*, the connecting link between the earth and the heavens, and the central axis around which all the universes revolve.

Leading off the courtyard is the *dukhang* (assembly hall), completed in 1459, containing a large throne for the Panchen Lama, watched over by the deities of universal compassion, Avalokiteshvara (Chenresi in Tibetan) and his reflex, the goddess Tara (Dolma), as well as the future Buddha, Maitreya (Jampa).

The story goes that a lama was dreaming of Jampa when the first Panchen Lama came into the hall, woke him and advised him that to create such a statue would bring great merit. A fund was set up. When the image was cast, a metre high, a miniature figure of Tsong Khapa appeared spontaneously at its right ear. In another vision two suns, one large and one smaller, flooded the *dukhang* with their light, indicating a second, larger image should be built. The huge Jampa figure in the Lamkhang Chenmo was duly constructed during the reign of the ninth Panchen. During its consecration ceremony, attended by all the great religious dignitaries, a flower suddenly sprouted from the statue's forehead and the whole place was enveloped in fine rain shot through with rainbows. Such, for those who believe, are the unmistakable signs of the blessing power of the Buddhas.

ABOVE AND RIGHT
The discarded boots of
novice monks of the
Gelugpa or 'Yellow Hat'
school; assembly for
the recitation of
scriptures in the
Dukhang, one of the
temples in the Lakhang
complex.

The Jokhang, Tibet
Tibet's Resilient Heart

AT THE HEART OF LHASA, most mythical of cities, lies the Jokhang, 'the House of Sacred Mystery'. Nearly all of Lhasa's old centre has been razed and rebuilt by the occupying Chinese army to house their brothels, but this, her most important shrine, continues to fulfill a role that sacred sites have always done in times of darkness. It stands as a source of hope for millions of oppressed and displaced people, the focus for their spiritual inspiration and tenacious sense of national identity. Somehow, the Jokhang survived the Cultural Revolution with considerable loss but only minor damage. Now under the rule of Chinese bureaucrats who view it as a museum of the primitive, but valuable as a lure to western tourists and foreign currency, the Jokhang somehow continues to radiate an atmosphere of extraordinary spiritual vitality that is absent from other major shrines. As such its importance to the fragile entity that is contemporary Tibet cannot be exaggerated.

From its beginnings the Jokhang was a magical place. In A.D. 640 Princess Wencheng, one of the daughters of the Emperor of T'ang China was married to the Tibetan king Songtsen Gampo. On her ceremonial arrival in the holy city one of her dowry chariots that was carrying a particularly revered image of the Buddha became stuck in the mud. Turning to the royal soothsayers to discover the meaning of such an inauspicious omen, the Princess was informed that the topography of Tibet resembled 'a demoness lying on its back'. Not only the fate of the image, but all the country's misfortunes were due to these natural formations of the land.

It was decided by the laws of Tibetan geomancy that a temple for the image be built in Lhasa which would 'peg down' the demoness at her heart, and that this temple would be surrounded by a succession of other temples, arranged in concentric squares that would tether the various parts of her body and subdue the outlying areas of the country that fell under her influence. The scheme was never realized in its entirety, but nonetheless the whole country was ordered on this general plan to be a protective *mandala* radiating outwards from Lhasa, the epicentre of which was the Jokhang.

It is through the rite of circumambulation that the pilgrim incorporates the power of the object or place into his own being. Lhasa is thus divided into three concentric circumambulatory paths: the *lingkor*, which encircled the old city in its entirety; the *barkor*, the most popular route which encloses the inner city including the Jokhang; and the *nangkor*, encompassing just the inner area of the Jokhang complex. On all these routes, marked out at regular intervals by whitewashed incense shrines emitting mists of aromatic juniper smoke, the pilgrims can be seen daily. Clad in everything from damasked silk to roughly patched cotton, they walk clockwise with unhurried yet focused attention, whirling prayer-wheels in their hands as they repeat the incessant OM MANI PEME HUNG, the great *mantra* of Chenresi, Lord

OPPOSITE AND THIS PAGE
In the Kyilkhor Til a monk holds a *khada*, a silk scarf to be offered to an image; prostration circumambulation of the Jokhang; prayers before the most sacred of the Buddha images in the Jowo Sakyamuni chapel.

Tibet's Resilient Heart

of Compassion. Some, who may have waited their entire life for this pilgrimage, cover the route by measuring their length time and again in ritual prostration, their bloodied hands and knees scantily bandaged for protection; others look so old one wonders if they have the strength to walk another step. But strength is the one thing the Tibetans have in abundance.

The straggling pilgrim lines converge in the courtyard of the Jokhang, to assemble under heavy flapping awnings appliquéd, black on white, with the eight sacred symbols of the faith. All face inwards to the shrine in rapt attention. There are women in black gowns fronted by the colourful horizontally striped aprons that denote their married status, their hair plaited with huge chunks of turquoise and ears and necks hung with nuggets of coral, amber or jade; haughty nomads from Kham with long hair braided in red silk bandanas and knee-high felt boots decorated in bright reds and greens. The variety of headgear – traditionally an indicator of status – is splendid: wide-brimmed stetsons and fur-lined conical hats with long ear-flaps embroidered with gold and silver thread jostle alongside dapper felt trilbys, turbans and lurid baseball caps. Here and there children scamper through the crowds, dodging in and out of the pillars. One of these is inscribed with the terms of the Sino-

RIGHT Pilgrims, some prostrating themselves, crowd into the entrance courtyard of the Jokhang, hung with awnings bearing sacred symbols.

Tibetan treaty of A.D. 822 that vowed eternal peace and mutual respect between the two independent nations. This undulating tide of humanity may be motley, but spiritually they are immaculate, lordly in their humble devotion.

The Jokhang itself is divided into three floors of labyrinthine passages, stairways and wall shrines leading to magnificent tiered roofs of gilded copper. Central to the complex is a courtyard at the back of which is the *sanctum sanctorum* housing Shakyamuni (Jowo Chempo in Tibetan, 'Wish-fulfilling Jewel'), a statue of the historical Buddha at a young age, sitting in the meditation posture. Though this is only an eighteenth-century replacement for Princess Wencheng's dowry gift, stolen during the 1717 sack of Lhasa, its power is considered no less, and the fact that it survived the ravages of the Cultural Revolution has only added to its status. Shakyamuni is the senior of the Four Light Emanating Deities, the most potent of the many power-objects housed here. Such images are empowered by the consciousness of many high lamas, which acts to free the spiritual energy dormant in matter, and are further quickened by the devoted attention of generations of believers, in accordance with the universal law that attention enlivens its object. Treated as living beings, they are the catalysts of miraculous transformation.

Row upon row of butter lamps reveal flickering glimpses of the numerous astral realms comprising the Tibetan pantheon. Fierce protective deities, eyes staring and fangs protruding from their gaping mouths, float weightless beside bejewelled *bodhisattvas* whose faces are wreathed in the most tranquil and compassionate of smiles, assuring the throng below them that all, in time, shall be well.

ABOVE AND RIGHT A brass *momento mori* recalls the Buddhist view that all things are impermanent; the view from the Jokhang roof across to the Potala Palace, traditional winter residence of the Dalai Lama.

Putuoshan, China
White Lotus Island

RISING OUT OF THE MISTS of the East China Sea, about a hundred miles and a twelve-hour ferry ride south of Shanghai, is Putuoshan, 'White Lotus Island'. This small outcrop, four miles long by one wide, is effectively an extended and pedestrianized national park, and as such a delightfully rural relief from much of the mainland. But Putuoshan is more than just a rare haven of tranquillity, for it is considered to be the earthly abode of one of China's most popular deities: Guanyin, Goddess of Mercy. Originally the male Chinese version of Avalokiteshvara, the supreme Mahayana *bodhisattva* of compassion, Guanyin was portrayed as a female from the time of the Ming Dynasty [1368 onwards]. Guanyin means 'the one who always hears sounds' (i.e. listens to prayers), and she is very popular among those women desirous of children. Another soubriquet, 'Guanyin of the Southern Seas', shows she is also particularly worshipped by sailors, fishermen and others whose livelihood depends on the sea.

The ferry finally docks on the southern tip of the island, beside the Southern Gate of Heaven, a magnificent three-legged structure topped with tiled roofs. Glimpsed through the mists that are endemic here, it is an atmospheric introduction to what must have been an astonishing place. For in times gone by the island boasted a community of four thousand monks and no secular structures could be built on its soil. The Cultural Revolution closed the religious foundations but slowly the place is recovering some of its former glory, and the monasteries and temples seem active and well cared for.

The highest point of the island, Foding Shan, 'The Buddha's Head Peak', is almost 1000 feet above sea-level and the Sacred Mountain of the East to Buddhists. The traditional way to the top is from the east at dawn, up the 'heavenly stairway' of a thousand steps, each carved with a lotus. The full route begins at the coast with Chaoyong Dong, 'The Voice of the Tide Cave', where many have seen visions of the goddess, surrounded by her characteristic aura of purplish light, gleaming amid the rainbowed spray of the sea against the rocks. Then on to Puji Si, 'The Front Temple', a magnificent five-storey *pagoda* dating from the fourteenth century. Perhaps inevitably, this is surrounded by pilgrim souvenir stalls, the most popular of which sell yellow cotton bags by the dozen to the well-organized tour parties, whose leaders bellow the story of the Lord of Silence through orange plastic megaphones. A mile or more further brings evidence that on Putuoshan the Guanyin cult merged with an older stratum of faith , the Chinese belief that sacred

'I asked the boy beneath the pines.
He said, "The master's gone alone
Herb-picking somewhere on the mount,
Cloud-hidden, whereabouts unknown."'

CHIA TAO, NINTH CENTURY A.D.

OPPOSITE AND THIS PAGE
Temple processions and fine decorative panels in the temple of Puji, Putuoshan.

White Lotus Island

mountains are the Abode of the Immortals, ancestral spirits whose chief blessing is the rain. Fayu Si, 'Temple of the Rain Law', commemorates this belief; its enamelled tiles rise charmingly amidst the surrounding tea plantations and gently swaying bamboo, whose rustling leaves seem to whisper benediction. The temple houses a fine statue of the goddess surrounded by splendid golden dragons; each April her annual festival is celebrated here.

And so to the stairway. This last part of the ascent was a great penance; devout pilgrims touched their heads to the stone

ABOVE AND RIGHT
Acts of devotion in the face of repression: a monk visits the Puji Si shrine, while circumambulatory processions still take place along the walkway beneath its upswept roof.

every three steps, and there was a gruesome custom of setting fire to the hands so that Guanyin was drawn to appear, mercifully to assuage the pain. Near the summit is the third of the Putuoshan's great shrines, Huiji Si, 'the Enlightenment Temple', but somehow the finale is not a fitting end to the climb. Perhaps it is because the actual peak is fenced off and crowned with an ugly brick example of public works department building; perhaps it is because the orange of monks is greatly outnumbered by the blue of naval uniforms, giving the place that same military feel which is never quite absent in so much of the mainland. The fact that one is constantly handing over entrance fees, and that many of the hotels blankly refuse to accept non-Chinese, adds to an ambivalent feeling the sensitive traveller can hardly avoid in this country.

But happily, the long return walk down the west side of the mountain restores a vision of China as romantic as any Song Dynasty scroll-painting. Paved walkways wind through outcrops of rock half hidden in swirling tendrils of mist, arched bridges over streams remind one of childhood willow-pattern tea-times with elderly relatives, and every so often the red, blue and gold of temples flashes through the deep green of pine forests. Far down below, finely etched fishing junks bob lightly here and there on the scintillating waves, and tiny islets radiate out into the distance like the ordered axes of a natural mandala. Perhaps the goddess is still lively here after all, you feel. At any rate, her home, combining as it does three archetypal symbols of the spirit – cave (immanence), mountain (transcendence) and island (stability amidst the flux of change) – is a place of considerable charm, and perhaps even of a gentle magic.

Koya-san, Japan
Return to the Source

DRIVING THROUGH THE SOFTLY rolling Eastern Mountains south of Osaka, the traveller is met by a land that epitomizes the stereotype of rural Japan. Verdant hills, famed for their springtime peonies and cherry blossoms, are sprinkled by waterfalls and dotted with miniaturized temples, whose cypress-bark roofs nestle among graceful pines. But this vision of Japan as a charming herbacious border set on the edge of the Mongolian steppes is not quite what it seems, for these secluded hills have long been the heartland of an esoteric Tantric Buddhism, characterized by the spiritual alchemy of prolonged meditation and magical intercourse with the primeval natural forces.

Once past Nara, the furthest south of a number of holy mountains is Koya-san, Japan's principal centre of the esoteric Shingon ('True Word') school, founded in A.D. 816 by a monk called Kukai. Sent by the Emperor to China to study Buddhism, Kukai (later known as Kobo-Daishi: 'The Great Master who Propagates the Faith') absorbed the Vajrayana, an esoteric Mahayana school practised in Tibet and Mongolia. Following his return Kukai sought to blend this teaching with Japan's Shinto beliefs, thereby purifying the state religion, by developing a reformed faith, grounded in first-hand mystical experience. The result was a system that relied strongly on ceremonial ritual, especially fire offerings to the presiding spirit energies, yet incorporated the traditional Buddhist relationship of *guru* and disciple in the arduous transformation of passions and ignorance on the way to *nirvana*. Sexual continence was an important means of generating and containing spiritual energy on this path; women have only been admitted to the mountain since 1872.

The seven million odd followers of Shingon consider all deities, including the *kami* spirits worshipped in Shinto, as the emanations of a supreme Buddha-nature called Rushana-butsu – the Japanese version of the central Vajrayana deity Vairochana. With the *kamis* in its pantheon, Buddhism, in Japan since the sixth century but unpopular because identified with foreign Chinese influence, was ready to enter the Japanese cultural bloodstream. It was to take two hundred more years for this syncretism between Shintoism and Buddhism to be completed, but it had been set in motion.

These new teachings were enshrined in a visionary art, totally different from the severely minimal Shinto aesthetic. Its central theme was the depiction of two complementary cosmic *mandalas*: Kongo-kai ('The Diamond World of Spirit') representing the Absolute Buddha-nature, and Taizo-kai ('The Womb World of Form') portraying the manifold relative worlds of time and space. Centred on Vairochana, the Buddha of Supreme Wisdom, there are realms of celestial or angelic beings (*ten*), and those of the infernal creatures (*oni*) dear to the darker reaches of the Japanese psyche: perpetually hungry ghosts (*gaki*) with huge bellies and long thin necks; angry spirits (*ashura*) with bird-like beaks and small wings and other sundry underworld spirits (*naraka*). Shingon heralded a renaissance in Japanese art which was to reach its

OPPOSITE AND THIS PAGE
Figures of Jizo, guardian of children, watch over tombs in Okuna-in cemetery on Koya-san; the shrine dolls include a figurine of Minnie Mouse.

ABOVE AND OPPOSITE
The *karahitsu* midday meal for the Kobo-Daishi deity, Torodo, Okuno-In; the monks first prepare the meal, then ritually bear it to the shrine, wearing masks so as not to defile it with their breath.

Return to the Source

peak in Koya-san's superb twelfth-century illustrations depicting the paradises associated with Amida, the Buddha of Boundless Light.

Kukai's project demanded solitude, silence and natural beauty, and in A.D. 816 the Emperor Saga granted him a site on Mount Koya-san, south-west of Kyoto and long holy to Shinto. The fledgeling Shingon brotherhood had to work hard, for the site was isolated and short of water. Added to which, it was far from commercial centres and their specialist building workshops, but at least there was abundant wood. The result of their labours was a new form of architecture. The monolithic Nara-style monastery, with its administrative offices, dormitories and cloisters, was too large and busy for prolonged deep meditation, and also physically unsuited to the new terrain. So it was now replaced by clusters of smaller buildings, discrete units staggered up the mountain side on small level terraces linked by elegant pathways and blended into the natural surroundings. The choice of a modular layout for the Koya-san complexes was also to limit their destruction in the event of fire, a perpetual concern in a country totally without a tradition of masonry architecture. A human and personal scale had been rediscovered, escalating by the late Middle Ages into a tremendous community. By the 17th century there were more than 1500 temple-monasteries scattered over the slopes of Koya-san, of which some 120 remain.

In building his main shrine, Kongobuji, 'Temple of the Diamond Peak', the indefatigable monk chose a spot surrounded by a corona of eight peaks that nicely mimic the eight petals of the Buddhist lotus. He set about developing a new form of *pagoda* that married the structure's Indian origin (the word *pagoda*

is a corruption of the Sanskrit *dhatu garbha*, meaning 'womb of relics', the name given to the Singalese *stupas* in the early years B.C.) to Japanese wooden buildings. This hybrid pagoda was known as the *taho-to*, 'pagoda of the treasures', and its inspiration was a fabled iron *stupa* in south India, reputed in Vajrayana tradition to have been filled with divinities, from whom, due to his piety and skilful recitation of key texts, the great patriarch Nagarjuna first received the Vajrayana scriptures.

The arrangement of the main Kongobuji buildings followed the dual mandalas: the Great Pagoda corresponding to the 'Diamond World' and the West Pagoda to the 'Womb World'. In the event, the original *taho-to* of Kukai's temple were destroyed by fire in A.D. 994 and only one rebuilt, most recently in 1938. But an original example of Kukai's innovative style can be seen here in the oldest extant structure, the Kongosammai-in temple [A.D. 1223]. Between two stepped roofs a simulated dome is inserted, from which attractive wooden bracketed consoles gracefully effect the transition to the square roof, creating a unique and attractive whole that well expresses the nature of the place: shaded and tranquil.

Kukai has become a national hero, and to this day none of the sixty-odd schools that comprise the byzantine complexity of Japanese Buddhism has produced a more attractive or influential personality. One of Japan's greatest calligraphers, he invented *hiragana*, a purely Japanese system of script free from Chinese ideograms.

So now he sits, enshrined as an emanation of Buddha Vairochana himself, in the cemetery of Okuno-in here on Koya-san. His mausoleum is surrounded by a vast graveyard, cradled in the Koya Ryujin forest, containing over 200,000 graves dedicated to ancient families of

repute. Pillars, obelisks and five-tiered *stupas*, which mark the resting place of an important *samurai* or court official, stand alongside modern corporate memorials. And then there are the row upon row of figures of Jizo, the Guardian of Children, watching over their charges.

The Master, who died in A.D. 835, is considered to be in perpetual meditation; locals speak of him as if he were still alive. Each morning, monks thread their way through this extraordinary necropolis, dappled by the shafts of sunlight that filter through the giant cedars. They carry food from the temple kitchens to be offered to his altar, their robes a startling orange.

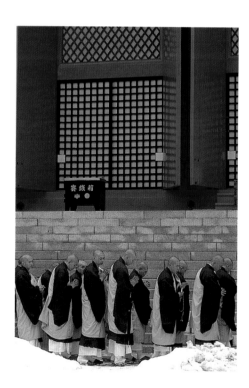

ABOVE AND RIGHT
Circumambulation at Garan temple, Koya-san; student monks recite scriptures in front of a lantern signifying the guiding light of Shingon.

A Note on the Photography

The idea for this book was conceived far from Asia, in the abandoned Inca city of Machu Picchu, in Peru. Over the years, I had completed many photographic projects on ancient sites around the world, most of them religious monuments of one kind or another. The themes have usually been architectural and art-historical, but what had begun to interest me was the underlying connection, their religious purpose. I was intrigued by what made this, and other places, sacred. Machu Picchu is dead, in the sense that it no longer has a religious life, or any real life; its population is a skeleton one of caretakers and a flow of tourists. Nevertheless, it is not hard to imagine how it must once have been, a spiritual focus of Inca society. The idea of conveying this through photography across a range of locations was attractive.

I began in Asia, where I have photographed regularly over the last twenty years, but with so many once and current sacred places, the matter of choosing sites and images dominated the two years over which most of the photography for this book was carried out. An early decision was to restrict the scope of this book to Eastern religions, and so not include Islam or Christianity; making a distinction, in other words, between sacred places of, rather than simply in, Asia. This was important because of the theme of place, which demanded the inclusion of centres of faith, where they exist.

There was then the issue of historical versus active sites of worship. The crowds of worshippers at Tirupati in southern India, for example, leave no doubt as to its sanctity, but what about the religious centres that time has passed by? At what point, if ever, does a once-sacred place lose its spirituality if it is abandoned? A few like Borobudur, Angkor and Pagan, are so important that they cannot be ignored, even though they now receive a trickle of the faithful. Many, many others, however, were left out, often with regrets, because they lacked the spiritual and visual energy imparted by active, current worship.

A growing number of ancient sites are, regrettably, having the sanctity leached out of them as they are turned into museums for the purpose of tourist revenue, and here I had no qualms about moving on. In contrast, some locations, such as Varanasi on the banks of the Ganges and the Shwedagon Pagoda in Burma, happily fulfill both criteria in that they have ancient pilgrims, with a corresponding wealth of art and architecture, while still drawing pilgrims, and these were among the rewarding places to visit. Nevertheless, faced with such an overwhelming choice, both of places and of the visual riches within each one, I had to perform a kind of photographic triage, leaving out many fine sites and concentrating on those that would contribute most to the essence of this book.

Photographically this has been an exploration, not simply of how places look and of their atmosphere, but of their importance to the people for whom they are or were sacred. Inevitably, in dealing with what have almost all been centres of pilgrimage, it has been an exploration of the mystery of faith. To this there are no simple or explicit answers, and for this very reason photography, which is necessarily oblique, has some advantages. It was a journey that took me to some extraordinary places: the world's highest lake, largest temple, most crowded place of pilgrimage, and more. All of this reflects the strength of faith which attaches to them. For the pilgrims each one is a locus of belief. I have no idea whether they contain an inherent, mysterious power, or have acquired their sanctity by sheer effort of worship, but the truth lies in the belief attached to them. At Mount Kailash, the most sacred of all of Asian mountains, a *sadhu* explained to Giuseppe Tucci, the most distinguished of this century's Tibetologists, 'God is here within us...and not there on the mountain: the mountain is no more than a heap of stones.' In the same way that the Buddha would steer disciples away from earthly attachments, the ascetic was debunking the natural splendour of this holy site to make an essential point, but for believers, such places shine. As we have tried to celebrate in his book, they are the mirrors of faith.

Michael Freeman

Glossary

Arati
Hindu worship of the image of the deity.

Ashram
Place of retreat where a guru instructs disciples.

Atman
The Self; pure Consciousness beyond the mind.

Avalokiteshvara
Mahayana *bodhisattva* of compassion.

Avatara
An incarnation of God, usually of Vishnu.

Bhagavad Gita
The most popular Hindu scripture.

Bhakti
Religious devotion.

Bodhi tree
Tree under which Buddha attained Enlightenment.

Bodhisattva
Celestial being who works for the Enlightenment of all.

Brahma
Hindu god embodying creative aspect of evolutionary process.

Brahman
Hindu term for ultimate Reality; source and goal of all phenomena.

Brahmin
Member of the priestly caste.

Chaitya
Buddhist temple in the form of a basilica.

Chakra
Energy centre in the subtle body.

Chedi
Thai word for *stupa*.

Chhattra
Royal parasol, finial of a *stupa*.

Chorten
Tibetan word for *stupa*.

Dagoba
Sri Lankan word for *stupa*.

Darshan
Sight of a deity, saint or holy place.

Dharma
The Natural Law that governs the universe.

Dharma chakra
The Wheel of the Law, symbol of Buddhist teaching.

Dukkha
The inherent dissatisfaction caused by the impermanence of life.

Ganesha
Elephant-headed Hindu deity, god of good beginnings.

Garbha griha
'Womb-house', holy of holies in Hindu temple.

Gautama
The Buddha's original name.

Gelugpa
Reform school of Tibetan Buddhism, the 'Yellow Hat'.

Gompa
Tibetan monastery-temple complex.

Guru
Spiritual teacher.

Guru Granth Sahib
Holy book of the Sikhs.

Guru Gobind Singh
Last of the ten Sikh *gurus*.

Hanuman
Hindu deity, monkey general of Rama.

Hinayana
'Little vehicle', popular name for Theravada Buddhism.

Hti
Spire of a Burmese *stupa*.

Jina
'Conqueror'; name for a Jain saint.

Kami
The spirits, including ancestors, worshipped in Shinto.

Karma
Universal law of action and reaction.

Lingam
Phallic emblem of Shiva.

Mahavira
Historical founder (6th century B.C.) of Jainism.

Mahayana
'Great Vehicle'; later Buddhism.

Mandala
Circular diagram of cosmos as meditational and teaching aid.

Mantra
Sound for use in meditation.

Moksha
Hindu name for Enlightenment, i.e. liberation in life.

Nirvana
Buddhist name for Enlightenment, i.e. liberation in life.

Nyingmapa
Original school of Tibetan Buddhism, the 'Red Hat'.

Padmasambhava
Teacher who took Buddhism to Tibet in the 8th century.

Pancharatna
'Five jewel' layout of many Hindu temples.

Pagoda
Burmese and Far Eastern name for *stupa*.

Parinirvana
Death of the Buddha.

Peepal (Eng: Peepul)
Tree (*ficus religiosa*) also known as the *bodhi*, or *bo*, tree.

Pradakshina
Circumambulation of sacred site, place or person.

Puja
Ritual worship.

Rupa
Buddhist image.

Sadhu
Wandering holy man.

Samsara
The never-ending round of relative existence, birth and death.

Sangha
Community of Buddhist monks.

Shakti
The Goddess; the feminine principle as primal creative energy.

Shakyamuni
'Sage of the Shakya clan', a name of the historical Buddha.

Shastra
Sacred scripture.

Shiva
Hindu god personifying transformative aspect of evolution.

Shunyata
Buddhist term for ultimate Reality, source and goal of all phenomena.

Stupa
Buddhist relic mound; originally hemispherical, later varied.

Sutra
Sacred scripture.

Tantra
Esoteric schools centred on *shakti* worship.

Thupa
Sri Lankan word for *stupa*.

Theravada
'Doctrine of the Elders', original Buddhism.

Tirtha
Place of pilgrimage or spiritual power.

Tirthankara
Enlightened teacher in Jain tradition.

Vajrayana
Mahayana schools teaching 'rapid path' to Enlightenment.

Vishnu
Hindu deity personifying maintenance of evolutionary process.

Vedas
Sacred scriptures of the Hindus.

Wat
A Thai or Cambodian temple complex.

Yoni
Female generative organ as symbol of *shakti*.

Yoga
Any systematic method of union with the Divine.

Yogi
One who practises *yoga*.

Yoni-lingam
Image combining male and female emblems, used in Shiva worship.

Zedi
Burmese word for *stupa*.

Select Bibliography

Dagens, Bruno (trans.), *Mayamatam*, Delhi, 1997.
Dowman, Keith, *The Power Places of Central Tibet*, London, 1988.
Eck, Diana, *Banaras– City of Light*, New York, 1982.
Felton, W. & Lerner, M., *Thai and Cambodian Sculpture*, London, 1989.
Le May, Reginald, *Buddhist Art in Siam*, Rutland, Vermont, 1977.
Levine, Norma, *Blessing Power of the Buddhas*, Shaftesbury, 1993.
Lowry, John, *Burmese Art*, London, 1974.
MacDonald, Malcolm, *Angkor*, London, 1961.
Michell, George, *The Hindu Temple*, London, 1977.
Miksic, John, *Borobudur, Golden Tales of the Buddhas*, London.
Ono, Sokyo, *Shinto– the Kami Way*, Rutland, 1997.
Pal, Pratapaditya (ed.), *The Peaceful Liberators*, London, 1996.

Rambach, Pierre, *The Art of Japanese Tantrism*, Paris, 1979.
Ramseyer, Urs, *The Art & Culture of Bali*, Oxford, 1977.
Rowland, Benjamin, *The Image of the Buddha*, London, 1978.
Shearer, Alistair, *The Hindu Vision*, London, 1993.
Shearer, Alistair, *The Traveller's Key to Northern India*, New York, 1989.
Shearer, Alistair, *Buddha: The Intelligent Heart*, London, 1977.
Strachan, Paul, *Pagan*, London, 1967.
Tucci, Giuseppe, *Tibet*, London, 1967.
Van Beek, Steve, *The Arts of Thailand*, Hong Kong, 1986.
Zimmer, Heinrich, *Myths & Symbols in Indian Art & Civilization*, Princeton, 1972.
Zimmer, Heinrich, *The Art of Indian Asia*, Princeton, 1983.

Acknowledgments

The photographer and publisher would like to extend special thanks to the following for their help in the preparation of this book:

Mr. Kaewkwan Vajorada, Lord Chamberlain of the Royal Court of Thailand; the office of the Superintendent of the Sanctuary, Ise-jingu, Japan.; the office of the Golden Temple, Amritsar, India; the Abbess of Gu Ni Gyaung, Sagaing, Burma; the Abbess of Zay Yar Theingi Gyaung, Sagaing, Burma; Yeang Sokhân, Siem Reap, Cambodia.